FAMILY AND CONSUMER SCIENCE 5
THE CLOTHES YOU SEW

CONTENTS

Author: Marcia Parker, M.Ed.
Editor: Alan Christopherson, M.S.
Illustrations: Alpha Omega Graphics

Alpha Omega Publications®

804 N. 2nd Ave. E., Rock Rapids, IA 51246-1759
© MM by Alpha Omega Publications, Inc. All rights reserved.
LIFEPAC is a registered trademark of Alpha Omega Publications, Inc.

THE CLOTHES YOU SEW

Sewing for yourself is not only fun and exciting, but also gives a sense of self-satisfaction. Whether you sew a garment to wear or create something for the home, your completed project will be an accomplishment.

Many small sewing tools were discussed in LIFEPAC® 4. Additional tools will be introduced in this LIFEPAC, along with a detailed description of the sewing machine and its parts. Sewing safety will also be addressed. Sewing skills will be developed in both hand and machine sewing techniques. This will prepare you for your sewing project and further develop your sewing skills notebook begun in LIFEPAC 4.

Choosing a pattern and your own perfect fabric will make your project unique. Once the techniques of layout, cutting, and marking are mastered, construction begins. With each step of construction, anticipation increases until the finishing touches of the completed garment or project.

> **Student:** You will continue working on your *Sewing Skills Notebook*. Reminder: fabric should be cut with pinking shears to prevent unraveling. Place glue on one edge of the fabric about ½″ to 1″ wide and stick it on its own sheet in the notebook. Leave the material loose on three sides so the teacher can check both sides of your sewing. Label each page with the name of the appropriate stitch or technique. For further organization, dividers may be added with the following names: Hand Stitches, Machine Stitches, Seams, Seam Finishes, Darts, Tacks, Pleats, Gathers, Hand-sewn Closures, and Machine-sewn Closures.

OBJECTIVES

Read these objectives. The objectives tell you what you will be able to do when you have successfully completed this LIFEPAC.

When you have finished this LIFEPAC, you should be able to:

1. Explain and demonstrate the use of small sewing tools.

2. Identify the parts of the sewing machine.

3. Understand and list basic sewing safety rules.

4. Demonstrate basic sewing techniques.

5. Select a pattern that is the correct size and style to flatter your figure.

6. Select fabric and notions appropriate for your pattern.

7. Interpret the pattern envelope, guide sheet, and pattern symbols.

8. Understand the layout and cutting of fabric.

9. Use a tracing wheel and tracing paper to transfer pattern markings from the pattern to the fabric.

10. Correctly press seams and darts.

11. Complete a sewing project which demonstrates the knowledge and skills learned.

I. SEWING EQUIPMENT

Gathering the supplies and getting started is always the hardest step in any project. Once you have set up a sewing station or corner of a room with the proper tools and equipment, you should be eager to start your project.

It is important to understand the use of each piece of equipment before you begin. A short review of sewing tools and their uses (including an in-depth study of the sewing machine) will begin this section, followed by a list of safety rules.

SECTION OBJECTIVES

Review these objectives. When you have completed this section, you should be able to:

1. Explain and demonstrate the use of small sewing tools.

2. Identify the parts of the sewing machine.

3. Understand and list basic sewing safety rules.

SMALL TOOLS

Of course, the first things that come to mind when you think of sewing are needles and thread. As mentioned in the previous LIFEPAC, it is good to have a variety of basic thread colors.

Needles. In addition to "sharps," hand sewing needles come in a variety of sizes, but should all be of good quality steel. The sizes range from 1-13; the larger the number the shorter and finer the needle. Needles are named for their intended purpose, fabric structure (whether knitted or woven), weight, and thread thickness. (See Chart *Types of Needles*) A needle should be fine enough to easily slip through fabric, yet heavy enough not to bend or break.

Types of Needles		
TYPES	**NAME**	**DESCRIPTION/USE**
General Hand Sewing: general purpose	Sharps	Most common. Medium length and round eye. Suitable for almost all fabric weights.
	Betweens	Also known as (aka) quilting needles.
	Milliners	Longer than others in this group. Useful for basting.
	Ball-points	Resemble sharps, except the point is rounded to penetrate between knit yarns.
	Calyx-eyes	Like sharps, except thread is pulled into a slot rather than an eye.

Needlecraft: embroidery, needlepoint, decorative beading, etc.	Crewels	Sharp, medium-length, used for embroidery. Long eye allows several strands of embroidery floss to be threaded.
	Chenilles	Sharp and heavy, used in yarn embroidery.
	Beading	Long and thin, for beading and sequin work.
	Tapestry	Heavy, with blunt points. Used for needlepoint and tapestry work.
Darning: Variety of lengths and diameters, accommodating most darning or mending jobs.	Cotton darners	Used to darn with fine cotton or wool.
	Double longs	Like cotton darners, but longer and able to span larger holes.
	Yarn darners	Long and heavy, necessary for yarn darning.
Heavy-Duty Sewing: Glover and sailmaker types have wedge-shaped points to pierce leather and leather-like fabrics in such a way that the holes resist tearing.	Glovers	Short, round-eye needles with triangular points that pierce leather, vinyl, or plastic without tearing.
	Sailmakers	Similar to glovers, except their triangular point extends part way up the shaft. For canvas and heavy leather.
	Curved needles	For upholstery, braided rugs, or lamp shades–anywhere a straight needle is awkward.

Sewing machine needles should be fine enough to penetrate the fabric without marring it, yet have a large enough eye that the thread does not fray or break. The sizes range from 9, a fine needle used for light-weight fabrics, to size 18 for heavy fabrics. The needle should be changed after it has been used to stitch two or three garments because it becomes bent or **burred** (rough-edged) from use.

There are a number of *straight pins* used for sewing. The longer the pin, the thicker it is. A *seamstress* or *silk pin* is suitable for light- to medium-weight fabrics. The standard length is $1^1/16''$. It is the most common pin and is the one suggested for your sewing/mending kit. There are also *pleating pins,* which are extra fine and used for delicate fabrics, and long pins used for heavy materials. There are different types of pin heads as well, the *flathead* being the most common. The *color ball* is easy to remove and see. The "T" is for heavy fabrics or very loose knit.

Scissors. Besides *sewing scissors* and *pinking shears*, there are two other handy types of scissors that you should consider adding to your kit. *Bent-handle dressmaker's* are the best for cutting out patterns, for they allow the fabric to lie flat because of the angle of the lower blade. Thus, they get a more even cut that follows the pattern the most accurately. They come in 6″ to 12″ lengths. Another handy pair of scissors to have are *embroidery scissors.* They are quite small and useful for not only embroidery, but for general needlework, ripping, clipping, and opening machine-stitched buttonholes.

Review the description and use for measuring devices (tape measure, seam, hem gauge, etc.) and sewing aids (thimbles, seam ripper, etc.) in LIFEPAC 4, Section IV. There are two other marking devices one should know how to use: *Tailor's chalk*, ideal for construction markings and fitting alterations; and a *tracing wheel* (with dressmaker's *tracing paper*) to transfer pattern markings.

Other sewing aids that you may consider adding to your kit are a *pin cushion* and extra **bobbins**, the spool-like thread holders that supply the bottom thread to sewing machines.

Answer the following questions.

1.1   Needles range in size from 1-13; the larger the number the _____ and _____ the needle.

1.2   Needles are named for their intended _____ , fabric _____ , weight and _____ thickness.

Match each phrase with the correct term.

1.3	_____ used for darning larger holes	a.	ball-points
1.4	_____ used in embroidering with yarn	b.	betweens
1.5	_____ thread is pulled into a slot rather than through an eye	c.	calyx-eyes
1.6	_____ quilting needles	d.	chenilles
1.7	_____ have triangular points to prevent tearing leather, vinyl or plastic fabrics	e.	curved needles
		f.	double longs
1.8	_____ rounded point so it can penetrate between knit yarns	g.	glovers
1.9	_____ most commonly used needle	h.	sharps
1.10	_____ used on upholstery		

Answer *true* **or** *false*. **If the statement is** *true* **write true in the blank. If the statement is** *false*, **change the underlined word or words to make the statement true. Write the correct answer in the blank.**

1.11 _____ A needle should be changed after it has been used to stitch <u>8–9</u> garments.

1.12 _____ The longer a straight pin is, the <u>thinner</u> it is.

1.13 _____ <u>Pleating pins</u> are used for delicate fabrics.

1.14 _____ The most common pin head is the <u>color ball</u> type.

1.15 _____ <u>Pinking</u> shears are the best for cutting out patterns.

1.16 _____ A <u>tracing wheel</u> is used to transfer pattern markings.

1.17 _____ <u>Tailor's chalk</u> is used for fitting alterations.

1.18 _____ The bobbin is a thread holder that supplies <u>the top</u> thread for the sewing machine.

SEWING MACHINE

There are many sewing machine types and brands, but they are all basically similar. The operating parts labeled on the machine shown are common to any average machine that does both straight and zigzag stitching. Placement of some items may differ based on the machine used.

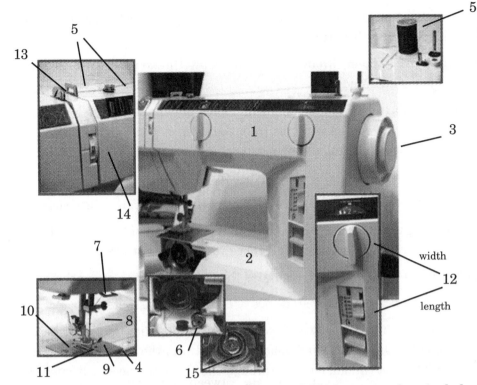

Each part has a specific function. The following list should help you understand the workings of a sewing machine better.

1. **head:** metal portion of the machine containing most of the mechanical parts
2. **bed:** the head's flat base which rests in the cabinet
3. **handwheel or balance wheel:** the wheel to the right of the upright section of the head, used in starting and stopping the machine
4. **slide plate:** the metal plate covering the **shuttle** (see #15)
5. **spool pin and thread guides:** the pieces which hold and guide the thread to be used as the upper thread in stitching
6. **bobbin:** the metal or plastic spool that the thread is wound around to be used as the lower thread in stitching
   It fits into a shuttle, filled with thread by means of a bobbin winder.
7. **needle bar:** holds the needle and carries upper thread down to it
8. **needle:** a needle with an eye and point at one end and a flat side on the other
   It is inserted into the needle bar and held in position with a clamp. It should be placed in the needle bar so that the flat side is in the groove and pushed up as far as it will go. The clamp screw is then tightened. If the needle is not in the correct position, the machine will not operate properly and the thread or needle will break.
9. **presser foot:** the piece which holds the fabric in place as you stitch raised and lowered by means of a lever called a presser-bar lever found on its back
   For stitching, the presser foot is lowered gently with the fabric in place and then raised to remove the fabric when the stitching is finished.
10. **throat plate:** the metal plate directly under the needle
    (In our illustration, this and #4 are united in one piece.)
11. **feed or feed dog:** the part which keeps the material moving as it is being stitched
    It is a tooth-like part located under the presser foot which projects upward through the throat plate.

12. **stitch regulator:** the device used for lengthening or shortening the stitch; there is another device for changing the width of the stitch

13. **take up lever:** a lever through which the upper thread passes, which moves up and down as the machine is operated

14. **tension regulator:** This device regulates looseness and tightness of stitches by controlling the pull on the thread as it comes from the needle. There is a similar tension on the lower thread of the bobbin, regulated by means of a screw on the bobbin case.

15. **shuttle:** the sliding container for the bobbin

    light: (not pictured) located on the bottom of the head, it illumines your view of your work

    pressure regulator: (not pictured) regulates the force of the presser foot as it holds the fabric layers in order to move them together evenly during stitching

    tension discs: (not pictured) regulates the tightness of the upper thread

    reverse button: (not pictured) device used to move the material backwards

Most home sewing machines are *locksmith machines*, meaning that they use two separate threads, one for the needle and one for the shuttle-and-bobbin assembly. As the machine sews, it interlocks the two threads in the fabric. The first thread, passing through the eye of the needle, is pushed through the fabric making a loop below. The bobbin thread is carried through the loop by a shuttle hook, "locking" the stitch.

Attachments. Many machines have attachments for sewing hems, zippers, buttonholes, and other details, although the newer computerized machines have the capabilities of completing these tasks without any extra attachments. Some machines have microprocessors enabling them to sew a number of stitches automatically. There is also a special machine called a *serger* that cuts and finishes seam edges, giving them a professional or store-bought look.

Threading. One process that might seem confusing is the upper threading of the machine. The parts of various machines may be in different locations with different appearances, but the upper progression of the thread is much the same. It is fed from the spool through the *tension discs* (which regulate the looseness and tightness of stitch), then to the take-up lever, and finally down to the needle. The number of thread guides between these points will vary with the machine.

down, into tension discs

Threading a sewing machine.

There are two important things to remember before threading any machine. First, raise the presser foot so the thread will be able to pass between the tension discs. Second, bring the take-up lever to its highest point so the needle will not come unthreaded when the first stitch is started. The instruction manual should give directions for threading the upper machine and the bobbin.

![spool icon] **Complete the following activities.**

Circle the sewing machine parts in the word search. Then match the part with the correct definition, description used below. Words may overlap or be written backwards.

```
F  S  S  L  I  D  E  P  L  A  T  E
K  D  E  A  N  I  P  L  O  O  P  S
N  E  T  A  L  P  T  A  O  R  H  T
G  R  N  E  S  L  P  F  R  E  D  I
A  H  E  C  O  E  R  E  E  V  I  T
N  E  E  D  L  E  E  V  E  T  C  H
O  Y  D  A  S  H  S  D  E  R  L  H
B  G  L  S  D  W  S  D  L  S  S  H
N  O  E  B  Z  D  U  O  P  E  H  C
R  R  B  E  D  N  R  G  U  B  U  L
P  H  A  B  L  A  E  S  E  U  T  I
B  O  R  E  I  H  Y  R  K  T  T  G
D  O  R  P  L  N  E  E  A  T  L  H
X  Y  M  N  T  O  P  U  T  O  E  T
S  C  S  I  D  N  O  I  S  N  E  T
```

1.19 The _____ is the portion of the sewing machine that rests on the cabinet.

1.20 The _____ is the portion of the sewing machine that contains most of the mechanical parts.

1.21 The _____ is the "thread holder" that has an eye and a point at one end and one flat side on the other end.

1.22 The _____ is the piece which holds the fabric in place as you stitch.

1.23 The _____ and the thread guides are the pieces that hold and guide the thread to be used as the upper thread in stitching.

1.24 The _____ is the piece that holds the needle and carries upper thread down to it.

1.25 The _____ is the metal plate directly under the needle.

1.26 The _____ is the tooth-like part that keeps the material moving as you stitch.

1.27 A _____ regulator regulates the length or width of a stitch.

1.28 The _____ is a metal or plastic spool that holds the lower thread for stitching.

1.29 The _____ is the bobbin case.

1.30 The _____ is the metal plate covering the bobbin case.

1.31 The _____ is the item used for starting and stopping the machine.

1.32 The _____ is the device that thread passes through and moves up and down.

1.33 The _____ is the device used to move material backwards.

1.34 The _____ regulates the amount of force the presser foot exerts on the fabric.

1.35 The _____ regulates looseness and tightness of stitch.

1.36   The _____ regulate the looseness and tightness of the upper thread.

1.37   The _____ , located on the bottom of the head, illumines the view of your work.

Complete the two demonstrations.

1.38   Point to and vocally name the parts of the sewing machine. Include all of the parts mentioned in the above activity.

1.39   Thread the sewing machine: both the upper and bobbin threads.

Adult Check   _____

                       Initial   Date

SAFETY

Just as there are important safety rules to obey in the kitchen, there are rules for sewing as well. Below is a list of the more important safety precautions while sewing.

1.   Put pins and needles in a pincushion, never in your mouth, on your clothes, or on upholstered furniture.

2.   Keep sharp objects out of your lap.

3.   Pass sharp objects such as scissors and shears to others handle first.

4.   Store scissors and other sharp objects in holders and other secure places.

5.   Keep blades of shears and scissors closed when not in use.

6.   While learning to operate an electric sewing machine, use the slow speed.

7.   Keep your fingers away from the path of the sewing machine.

8.   Do not touch the hot light bulb on the sewing machine.

9.   Keep the machine's electric cord on the floor so that it will not cause anyone to trip.

10.   Disconnect the cord from the outlet before disconnecting it from the machine.

11.   Close the sewing machine carefully to avoid damaging the electric cord.

12.   Keep the drawers or doors of the sewing machine storage cabinet closed to avoid bumping into them.

13.   When pressing, keep your hands away from the steam. Turn off the iron when not in use to avoid accidental burns. An unattended hot iron is a fire hazard.

14.   Never stand on a chair while measuring the hem of a garment.

Always practice safety.

8

Complete the following activity.

1.40 Read the following paragraph about Calamity Claire's sewing experience and complete the question that follows.

Calamity Claire decided she needed to shorten a skirt. Her mother carefully measured the new hem line for her. As Calamity jumped down from the chair, she ran into the cabinet drawer she had forgotten to close previously, when she got straight pins out. Ouch! When she finally sat down to the sewing machine to stitch the hem, she nearly stitched her fingers as well as the skirt. OOPS! Calamity carefully removed the pins from the material as she stitched so that the machine needle would not hit one and break, sticking them in the lapel of her jacket so that none would fall on the floor. When she finished sewing, she carefully took the scissors from her lap and cut the end threads. As she got up to go press the hem, she tripped over the sewing machine cord. While pressing the new finished hem, she burned herself with the iron's steam. Ouch! Calamity was relieved to have the project done and promptly unplugged the cord from the machine before pulling it from the outlet. She put her skirt on and rushed out the door, leaving the iron on. With a slight limp, burned hand and straight pins still clinging to her jacket, Calamity Claire was quite proud of her accomplishment.

Calamity Claire

Which safety rules did Calamity Claire forget?

a. _____

b. _____

c. _____

d. _____

e. _____

f. _____

g. _____

h. _____

i. _____

Review the material in this section in preparation for the Self Test. The Self Test will check your mastery of this particular section. The items missed on this Self Test will indicate specific areas where restudy is needed for mastery.

SELF TEST 1

Answer *true* or *false* (each answer, 3 points).

1.01 _____ Tension discs and thread guides control the flow of threads.

1.02 _____ The presser foot moves the fabric as you stitch.

1.03 _____ The balance wheel is used for starting and stopping the machine.

1.04 _____ The sewing machine will not operate properly if the needle is not in correct position.

1.05 _____ The bobbin controls the pull on the thread as it comes from the needle.

Matching (each answer, 5 points).

1.06 _____ keeps material moving toward the back of the machine while stitching

1.07 _____ holds fabric in place while you stitch

1.08 _____ device used for lengthening or shortening the stitch

1.09 _____ spool which holds the lower thread used in stitching

1.010 _____ metal plate directly under the needle

1.011 _____ regulates looseness and tightness of stitch

1.012 _____ holds the needle

a.   bobbin

b.   feed dog

c.   needle bar

d.   presser foot

e.   spool pin

f.   stitch regulator

g.   tension regulator

h.   throat plate

Match the correct letter of the sewing machine part by its correct name (each answer, 5 points).

1.013 _____ bobbin case

1.014 _____ feed dog

1.015 _____ handwheel

1.016 _____ presser foot

1.017 _____ light

1.018 _____ stitch length regulator

1.019 _____ stitch width regulator

1.020 _____ tension regulator

1.021 _____ thread take-up lever

1.022 _____ throat plate

<table>
<tr><td>80</td></tr>
<tr><td>100</td></tr>
</table>

Score _____

Adult Check _____

Initial   Date

Hand sewing skills are vital to develop, even in this modern day of technology. You never know when you will not have a sewing machine or electricity available. Knowing how to sew by hand may be your only method for mending and/or sewing clothes.

Although you learned some basic hand-stitches in LIFEPAC 4, this section will review some of those and introduce new stitches for you to master. This section will also give you the opportunity to learn and practice several machine stitches and specialty techniques used in sewing various garments.

SECTION OBJECTIVE

Review this objective. When you have completed this section, you should be able to:

4. Demonstrate basic sewing techniques.

HAND STITCHES

Even backstitches are the strongest backstitches. They look much like machine stitching; that is, they are even in length with very little space between them. They are used mainly to make and repair **seams**. You should already have a sample of backstitching in your *Sewing Skills Notebook*.

Basting is a long, straight stitch used to temporarily hold fabric layers together during fitting and construction. *Even basting* consists of short, temporary stitches made the same distance apart on smooth fabrics that need more control when being stitched on a machine. Examples are: curved seams, seams with ease, and set-in sleeves. *Uneven basting* is used for general basting on edges that require less control during permanent stitching. Two examples are straight seams as found on side or shoulder seams.

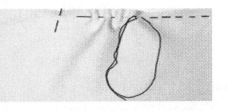 

Even basting: Working from right to left, take several short (about ¼″ long) evenly spaced stitches into the fabric before pulling the thread through.

Uneven basting: Similar to even basting, take short, temporary stitches (about ¼″ long) which are about 1″ apart.

Hemming stitches are used to secure hem edges to a garment. The steps for hemming a garment are as follows. 1) Measure and mark the desired length for the finished garment. 2) Fold the raw edge back ¼″–½″ (or finish the edge by pinking, sewing a zigzag or straight stitch, or applying hem tape to it). Press. 3) Fold back again to the marked desired finished length. 4) Pin in place. Make sure the material is evenly distributed so that the hem lays flat without bunching. 5) Stitch by hand or machine. Hand stitches should be ⅜″–½″ apart and invisible on the outside. Press. If you use a sewing machine for blind-hemming, the stitch pattern consists of 4-6 straight stitches followed by one zigzag stitch. Be careful to make sure the zigzag stitch just barely catches the fabric, but does not grab too much so that it shows badly on the outside. Hem stitches for your *Sewing Skills Notebook* were completed in LIFEPAC 4.

There are four basic standards for determining the quality of a hem: 1) Hangs parallel to the floor. 2) Stitches don't show on the outside. 3) Clean, finished raw edge. 4) Appears flat and smooth from the outside.

A *running stitch* is a very short, even stitch used for fine seams, tucking, mending, gathers, and other delicate sewing. The running stitch is like even basting except that the stitches are smaller and usually permanent.

A *blanket stitch* is a decorative edge finish formed by looped interlocking stitches. It is traditionally used for embroidery or a decorative edge. It is also used in making a bar tack (see tacks below).

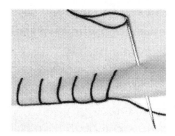

Blanket Stitch: Working from left to right with the point of the needle and the edge of the work toward you. Secure thread and bring out below edge. For the first and each succeeding stitch, insert the needle through the fabric from the right side and bring it out from the back at the edge and up through the thread from the previous stitch. Draw the needle and thread through it.

Tacks are hand stitches done during construction or for marking. *Construction tacks* are stitches used to join areas that must be held together without a seam, or as a reinforcement at points of strain. For example, a bar tack is a straight reinforcement tack used at points of strain such as buttonhole ends or pocket corners. *Marking tacks* are used to transfer construction details and matching points from the pattern to fabric sections. These are alternatives to marking pens, chalk or tracing paper. For example, a *tailor's tack* is a marking tack used to transfer individual pattern symbols, (such as dots) to double layers of fabric.

Note: Keep the sides of your fabric distinct. The **right** side of the fabric is the side that will be seen. The **wrong** side is the side which will remain unseen.

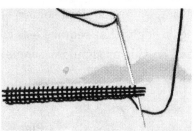

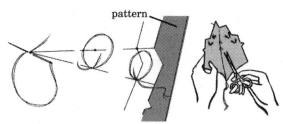

pattern

Bar Tack: Fasten thread to needle then bring needle through to right side. 1. Make two or three long stitches (the length that the bar tack is to be) in the same place. 2. Catching the fabric underneath, work enough closely spaced blanket stitches around the thread to cover it.

Simplified Tailor's Tack: Using a long length of double unknotted thread, make a small stitch on the pattern line through the pattern and the fabric. Pull the needle and thread through, leaving 1″ thread ends. Make similar stitches where needed to sufficiently mark your fabric. Gently lift the pattern off the fabric, taking care not to pull out the thread marking.

Complete the following exercises.

2.1   The _____ is used mainly to make and repair seams.

2.2   _____ is used to temporarily hold together two or more fabric layers during fitting and construction.

2.3   Give an example of when you would use even basting. _____

2.4   Give an example of when you would use uneven basting._____

2.5   List the steps in hemming a garment. Give the measurements or explain how to figure them.

     a. _____

     b. _____

     c. _____

     d. _____

     e. _____

2.6   What stitch is similar to an even basting stitch except smaller and permanent? _____

     _____

2.7   Describe the two steps used to make a bar tack.

     a. _____

     b. _____

2.8   What kind of tack is used to transfer pattern symbols?_____

Complete the following activities.

2.9   Baste a *seam*. Cut a 6″ square piece of fabric. Fold in half and stitch the open seam together using an *even basting* stitch, ⅝″ from the open edge. Glue the folded edge of the piece of fabric into your *Sewing Skills Notebook*.

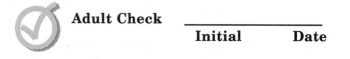

        Adult Check _____

                     Initial   **Date**

2.10   Baste a *seam*. Cut a 6″ square piece of fabric. Fold in half and stitch the open seam together using an *uneven basting* stitch, ⅝″ from the open edge. Glue the folded fabric edge of the piece of fabric into your *Sewing Skills Notebook*.

        Adult Check _____

                     Initial   **Date**

2.11   Use the blanket stitch in making a *bar tack*. Cut a 3″ square piece of fabric and sew a *bar tack* on it. Glue one edge of the piece of fabric into your *Sewing Skills Notebook*.

        Adult Check _____

                     Initial   **Date**

2.12   Make a *tailor's tack*. Cut a 3″ square piece of fabric and sew a tailor's tack on it. Glue one edge of the piece of fabric into your *Sewing Skills Notebook*. Both tacks can be placed on the same page of your notebook.

        Adult Check _____

                     Initial   **Date**

MACHINE STITCHES

A *backstitch* is used to secure the beginnings and ends of machine stitching rows, which eliminates the need to tie the thread ends. However, it should not be used to secure areas such as the tapered end of a dart (see DARTS in next section) because reversing the stitching direction can distort the fabric. When a backstitch is not appropriate, tying the thread ends is another method to secure the ends of machine stitches. It is not as strong as backstitching, but it is a neater finish. Simply bring the lower thread through to the other side of the fabric. Pull the upper thread to start the lower, then pull it through completely. Tie the thread together using a square knot, and trim away the excess thread ends.

Basting is produced by setting the straight stitch at the longest available length, 6 per inch. Since basting is usually a temporary stitch, do not backstitch at either end.

The *blind-hemming* stitch (aka *blind stitch*) is a zigzag pattern used primarily for blind-hemming by machine. It can also be used to stitch seams or as a seam finish. The stitch pattern consists of 4-6 straight stitches followed by 1 single zigzag stitch. This skill was developed in LIFEPAC 4.

The *overcast* stitch is any machine stitch that forms over the raw edge of the fabric in order to avoid raveling; simple zigzag is the most common. Position the fabric so stitches will form over the edge; or stitch and then trim away the excess fabric. Its most basic applications are for narrow seams and seam finishes.

Top-stitching is machine stitches done on the right side for decorative and functional reasons. Most often you use the plain straight stitch, set at a longer than usual stitch length. The thread can match or contrast the garment. Sometimes a double row or zigzag is preferred. Tie the thread ends.

Under-stitching is a straight stitched line applied to facing seams (see FACINGS), to keep their **allowances** (distance between the cutting line and the seam line) lying flat in a particular direction. **Trim**, **grade**, and **clip** all seam allowances, then press to the side where the under-stitching will be placed. Straight stitch on the right side close to the seam line through all fabric layers and allowances.

Complete the following activities.

2.13   What two ways can be used to secure the beginings and the ends of machine stitching rows? ___

_____

2.14   Which method is best used in securing the thread ends of a dart?_____

2.15   As mentioned in the previous section, what is the use of a basting stitch? _____

2.16   The machine stitch length used for basting is _____ .

2.17   The blind-hemming stitch consists of _____ straight stitches followed by _____ zigzag stitch(es).

2.18   The most basic application for the overcast stitch is for _____ seams and seam _____ .

2.19   What is the purpose of under-stitching? _____

2.20   Define grading with reference to seam allowances. _____

 **Answer** *true* **or** *false*.

2.21   _____ Backstitch all basting stitches.

2.22   _____ Top-stitching is done on the right side of the garment.

2.23   _____ When top-stitching, secure thread ends by backstitching.

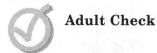 **Complete the following activities.**

2.24   Machine sew a *basting stitch*. Cut a 6″ square piece of fabric. Fold in half and baste a ⁵/₈″ seam. Be sure to start and stop the machine using the handwheel and go very slowly if you have never sewn with a machine before. Watch your fingers. Do not backstitch or tie thread ends. Glue the folded edge of the fabric into your *Sewing Skills Notebook*.

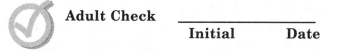

         Adult Check _____
                Initial   **Date**

2.25   Machine sew an *overcast* edge on a seam. Cut a 6″ square piece of fabric. Fold in half, sew a ⁵/₈″ seam. Finish the seam edge with an overcast zigzag stitch. Glue one edge of the fabric into your *Sewing Skills Notebook*.

         Adult Check _____
                Initial   **Date**

2.26   Machine sew a *topstitch*. Cut a 6″ square piece of fabric. Fold in half and sew a ⁵/₈″ seam. Press the seam open. Turn the fabric right side out. Press the fabric so that the seam is centered between the folds. Using a contrasting color of thread, top-stitch ¹/₄″ each side of the seam line of the fabric. Check your presser foot. Some are ¹/₄″ from the outside of the foot to the needle for easy guidance. Glue the piece of fabric into your *Sewing Skills Notebook*.

         Adult Check _____
                Initial   **Date**

2.27   Machine sew an *under-stitching*. Cut a 6″ square piece of fabric. Now cut a 2″ strip from the 6″ square piece of fabric. Place the 2″ piece of fabric under the 6″ piece of fabric matching the edges on one side and the two ends. Sew a ⁵/₈″ seam. Grade the seam allowance. Press all seam allowances toward the 2″ piece of fabric (which now serves as a facing). Sew a straight stitch close to the seam allowance of the 2″ facing and through the allowances under it. Press the facing folded under. Glue the free edge of the fabric into your *Sewing Skills Notebook*.

SEAMS AND SEAM FINISHES

The *seam* (where two pieces of fabric are sewn together) is the basic structural element in any garment, and must be formed with care. Machine tension, pressure, stitch length, and the thread itself should be adjusted to the type of fabric used. A seam is usually formed by matching right sides of fabric pieces together and sewing a ⅝″ width. However, wrong sides are sometimes matched and various seam widths occasionally used. Check your pattern for any necessary special seam finishes and widths. All seams should be backstitched at the beginning and end for reinforcement.

In a well-made *straight seam*, the stitching remains exactly the same distance from the edge down the entire length of the seam. It may be used for any fabric. However, for stretchy fabrics, a tiny zigzag or special machine stretch stitch may be necessary.

A *curved seam* requires careful guiding so that the entire seam line will remain the same even distance from the edge. The two types of curved seams are *clipped* and *notched*. Each type requires a different trimming technique. The outward curved seam requires a notched edge so that excess material can be removed to prevent bunching. The inward curved seam requires a clipped edge. The slits or clips cut into the seam allowance permit the edges to spread. Take extra care not to clip or notch too deep into the allowance, cutting or weakening the stitching.

clipped   notched

One other type of allowance is the *cornered seam*, used in making collars, cuffs, and lapels.

Cornered seam.

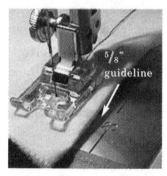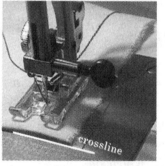

Step 1: Stitch a straight seam along the ⅝″ guideline found on the throat plate.

Step 2: When the edge of the material reaches the cornering crosslines on the slide plate, stop.

Step 3: Raise the presser foot. **Pivot** the fabric on the needle, bringing its bottom edge in line with the throat plate's ⅝″ guideline.

Step 4: Lower the presser foot and stitch in the new direction.

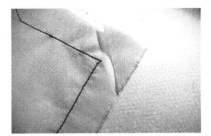

To trim a cornered seam, trim the seam allowances across its point, close to the stitching and taper them on either side.

When selecting a finish for your seam, consider these three things.

1. The type and weight of fabric; does it ravel?
2. What kind of wear and care will the garment receive? Wash and wear types must be durable.
3. Will the seams be seen? An unlined jacket needs an elaborate finish. Plain *straight* seams are finished after they are pressed open. Plain *curved* or *cornered* seams are seam-finished right after stitching, clipped or notched, and then pressed open.

The simplest finish is the *pinked edge*. Simply cut along the edge of the seam allowance with pinking shears. It is attractive, but will not prevent raveling by itself. It is well used on fabrics such as knits that are less apt to ravel.

The *stitched and pinked edge* is also quite simple and will minimize raveling. Short stitch a line of stitching ¼″ from the edge of the allowance, then pink the edge. When pinking, be careful to not cut the stitching.

The *zigzag* is one of the most effective seam finishes. Set the stitch for medium width and short length. Stitch near, but not on, the edge of the allowance. Be careful on knit materials because a stretched seam will not lie flat and will be ripply under the garment.

Self enclosed seams are those in which all allowances are contained within the completed seam, avoiding the need for a finish. They are used in garments that have more visible seams such as with sheer materials and unlined jackets. The *French seam* is the classic seam for sheers. It is stitched twice, once from the right side and once from the wrong side, and looks best if the finished width is ¼″ or less. The decorative *flat-felled seam* is very sturdy and is often used for sports clothing and children's wear.

French seam. Note: In this and future diagrams, the *wrong* side may be depicted in gray.

allowance

stitching

Step 1: a. Stitch *wrong* sides together using a ⅜″ seam allowance.
　　　　　b. Trim to ⅛″.
　　　　　c. Press seam open.

Step 2: a. Fold *right* sides together, with stitched line exactly on the edge of the fold.
　　　　　b. Press again.
　　　　　c. Stitch on the seam line, which is now ¼″ from the fold.
　　　　　d. Press seam to one side.

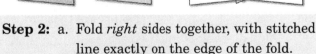

17

Flat-felled seam.

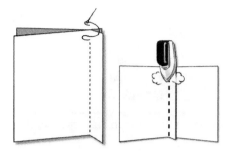 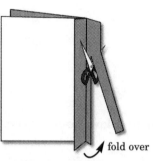 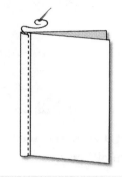

fold over

Step 1: With wrong sides together, stitch on the seam line (⁵/₈″). Press it open, then to one side.

Step 2: Trim the inner seam allowance to ¹/₈″. Press under the edge of the outer seam allowance of ¹/₄″.

Step 3: Stitch this folded edge to the garment. Be careful to press like seams in the same direction (for example, both shoulder seams should be pressed toward the front).

Proper seam finishes give garments a neat and professional appearance anyone can be proud of.

Answer *true* **or** *false*.

2.28 _____ All seams are made by matching right sides of the fabric pieces together.

Complete the following activities.

2.29 Seams are usually sewed at a _____ width, unless otherwise specified by the pattern.

2.30 An outward curved seam requires a _____ edge and an inward curved seam requires a _____ edge.

2.31 What three things should be considered in choosing a seam finish?

a. _____

b. _____

c. _____

2.32 Which seam finish is best for knit fabrics? _____

2.33 Which seam finish is the most effective? _____

2.34 The _____ seams are those in which all seam allowances are contained within the completed seam. Name two types. _____

Complete the following activities.

2.35 Machine sew and finish an *inward curved* seam. Cut a 6″ square piece of fabric. Fold in half and cut an outward curved edge on the fabric's open edge. Stitch the curved edge with a ⁵/₈″ seam allowance. Backstitch the beginning and end of the seam for reinforcement. Notch the allowance. Glue the folded edge of the fabric into your *Sewing Skills Notebook*.

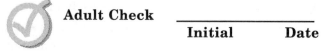 **Adult Check** _____

 Initial   Date

2.36 Machine sew and finish an *outward curved* seam. Cut a 6″ square of fabric. Fold in half and cut an inward curved edge on the open edge of the fabric. Stitch the curved edge with a ⁵/₈″ allowance. Back stitch the beginning and end of the seam for reinforcement. Clip the allowance. Glue the folded edge of the fabric into your *Sewing Skills Notebook*.

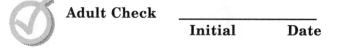 **Adult Check** _____

 Initial   Date

2.37 Machine sew and finish a *cornered* seam. Cut a 6″ square piece of fabric. Fold in half. Stitch a ⁵/₈″ seam allowance across the open edges; top, side and bottom. Trim the corners. Glue the folded edge of the fabric into your *Sewing Skills Notebook*.

Adult Check _____

 Initial   Date

2.38 Finish the following seams. For each, take a 6″ piece of fabric and cut it in half. Follow the steps given in the text; sew and finish a seam allowance for each of the following:
  ✂ pinked finish
  ✂ stitched and pinked finish
  ✂ zigzag finish
  ✂ French seam
  ✂ flat-felled seam
Press each seam open or to the side as specified. Glue one edge of the fabric for each of the seams sewn onto a separate page of your *Sewing Skills Notebook*.

 **Adult Check** _____

 Initial   Date

DARTS, TUCKS, PLEATS, GATHERINGS, AND FACINGS

In LIFEPAC 4, you learned that there are specialty stitches used in the construction of garments which help define a style or design. This is how you construct them.

The **dart** is a short, tapered, stitched area that enables the garment to fit the figure. It most often occurs at the bust, back, waist, and hips. It is important that the position be accurate if it is to gracefully emphasize these lines. Therefore, precisely marking construction symbols is extremely important. A dart is stitched from the wide end to the point. It is stitched straight and to a very fine point to prevent puckering. Backstitching can be used at the wide end, but the threads should be tied at the point. Press toward the point, but do not go beyond it because the garment could crease. Press according to the direction it will take in the finished garment.

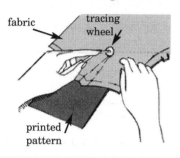
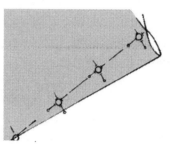
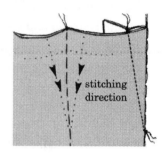

Step 1: Before removing the pattern, mark the wrong side of fabric.

Step 2: With right sides together, match and pin the markings.

Step 3: Starting from the wide end of the dart, stitch straight, no curves, to a very fine point. End the dart by sewing right off the material. Backstitch at the wide end and tie the threads at the point. Press.

A *contoured dart* is a long, single dart that fits at the waistline and then tapers off in two opposite directions to fit either the bust and hip (front contour dart) or the fullest part of both the back and the hip (back contour dart).

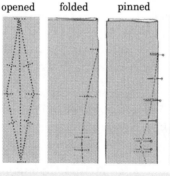
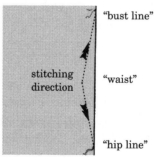

Step 1: Transfer the markings from the pattern onto the wrong side of the fabric.

Step 2: Fold dart right side together. Match and pin stitching line, starting at the waist then at both points. Baste and remove pins.

Step 3: Begin stitching at the "waist" and stitch toward the "bust line" point. Repeat this step, going from the waist to the "hip line" point. Use overlap stitching at the waist. Tie thread ends at both points of the dart.

Step 4: Clip at waistline within 1/8" of the stitching. Press dart toward center seam.

20

A **tuck** is a stitched fold of fabric (either inside or outside) that is typically decorative but also can be a shaping device. A tuck is formed by matching and stitching two lines; the fold of the tuck to the stitching line produces its width. Those that meet are called *blind tucks* and those with space between them are called *spaced tucks*. *Pin tucks* are very narrow.

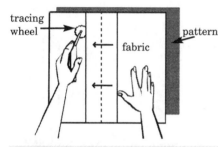
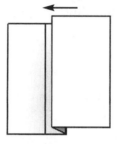
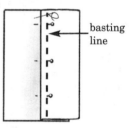

Step 1: Using tailor tacks, mark the stitching lines of each tuck according to your pattern.

Step 2: Remove your pattern. Fold the material, matching up the stitching lines, pin and baste along them.

Step 3: Stitch the tuck.

Pleats are folds in fabric which provide controlled fullness. They may occur as a single pleat, a cluster, or around an entire garment section. Most are formed by folding a continuous piece of fabric onto itself. There are several different styles: side (knife), box, inverted, accordion, and those with a separate underlay.

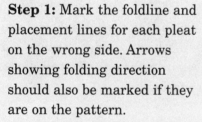

Step 1: Mark the foldline and placement lines for each pleat on the wrong side. Arrows showing folding direction should also be marked if they are on the pattern.

Step 2: Remove the pattern. Fold each pleat along its foldline to align with the placement line.

Step 3: Pin and baste.

Gathering is pulling fabric along a stitch line into a small area in order to create soft, even folds. The fabric is usually gathered to ¹/₃ or ¹/₂ its original width. This isn't done until the construction seams have been stitched, seam-finished, and pressed. Stitch length for gathering is longer, the tension looser, and the bobbin thread is pulled.

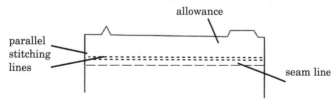

Step 1: On the right side of the fabric, stitch two parallel rows in the seam allowance. One should be just above the seam line and the other ¹/₄″ above the first.

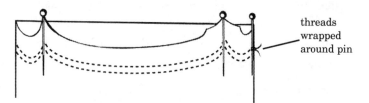

Step 2: Pin the stitches together on their right sides, being sure the notches, center lines, and seams match. Anchor one end of the bobbin threads by wrapping both around the end pin.

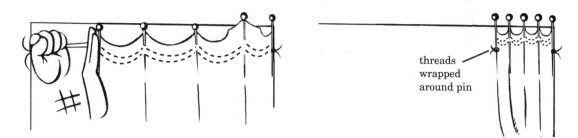

Step 3: Gently pull on the bobbin threads while sliding the fabric the other way with the other hand, creating uniform gathers. Secure gathered sections with pins. When the gathering is even and meets the end of the parallel stitch, secure the threads by winding them around a pin at this end.

Step 4: Baste the seam, removing the pins as you sew.

Step 5: Stitch the seam.

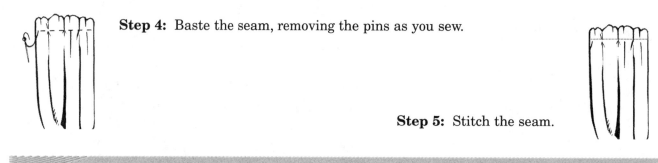

A **facing** is the fabric used to finish raw edges at garment openings such as the neck, armhole, front, or back openings. It can be a separate piece of fabric or part of the main piece which is folded. Blouse front openings often have a folded facing whereas necklines and armholes use separate facings. The techniques listed (which apply to a neckline) are the same ones used for several other facings.

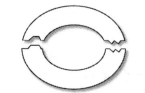

Step 1: Interface the front and back neck facings to match the instructions on your pattern.

Step 2: Pin the facing sections together, matching the notches. Stitch only the notched edges. Press seams open.

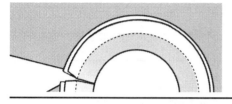

Step 3: On the outer edge (the one without notches), turn under ¼″ and press. On the right hand side of the fabric, edge stitch close to the folded edge.

Step 4: Pin the facing (with the right sides now stitched together) to the neck. Match the notches, shoulder seams and center front. The facing will extend ⅝″ past the back neck edge if a zipper has already been applied.

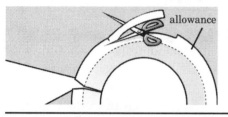

Step 5: Stitch along the seam line between the facing and the neck ⅝″ from the inside edge.

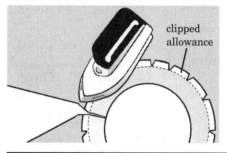

allowance

Step 6: Grade the seam allowance by first trimming the interfacing one. Then, trim the facing seam allowance to ⅛″. Finally, trim the garment seam allowances to ¼″.

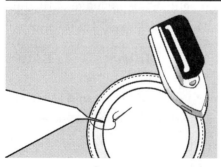

clipped allowance

Step 7: Clip the allowance about every inch around the neck edge, being careful not to clip through the stitching. Press the facing and seam allowances away from the garment.

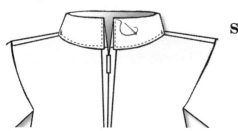

Step 8: Under-stitch the seam allowances to the facing. Turn and press the facing to the inside of the garment.

Step 9: To finish a facing edge by a zipper, turn the raw edges under. Fold the facing down over the zipper tape and hand stitch in place. With a few hand stitches, stitch the facing to the shoulder seams to keep it in place.

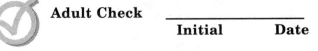

Complete the following activities.

2.39 Define dart. _____

_____

2.40 A dart is stitched from the _____ end to the _____ .

2.41 How do you reinforce the ends of a dart? _____

2.42 Define tuck. _____

2.43 What is the difference between a blind tuck and a spaced tuck. _____

_____

2.44 Define pleat. _____

2.45 Define gathering. _____

2.46 Which thread is pulled in gathering? _____

2.47 What is the purpose of a facing? _____

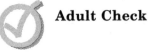

Complete the following activities.

2.48 Make a *regular dart*. Cut a 6″ square piece of fabric. Follow the instructions given in the text. Sew a dart 4″ in length, starting ¹/₂″ in width. Backstitch at the beginning and tie threads at the end point. Glue one edge of the fabric into your *Sewing Skills Notebook*.

 **Adult Check** _____
                                                      Initial   **Date**

2.49 Make a *contour dart*. Cut an 8″ square of fabric. Fold the fabric in half. Mark the center of the fold as the center of your dart. Stitch from the center to a point ¹/₂″ from the edge of the fold at each end. Continue according to the instructions given in the text. Secure and clip. Glue one edge of the fabric into your *Sewing Skills Notebook*.

Adult Check _____
                                                      Initial   **Date**

2.50 Sew by sewing five evenly spaced *pin tucks*. Cut a 6″ square piece of fabric. Measure and stitch the tucks on the right side. Press to one side and hold in place with a basting stitch. Glue one edge of the piece of fabric into your *Sewing Skills Notebook*.

Adult Check _____
                                                      Initial   **Date**

2.51 Connect a *gathered section* of material to a flat piece of material. Cut one 6″ square piece of fabric and one 3″ square piece of fabric. Stitch two rows of gathering at the top of the 6″ square of fabric. Continue by following the directions given in the text. Glue one edge of the piece of fabric into your *Sewing Skills Notebook*.

Adult Check _____
                                                      Initial   **Date**

CLOSURES

Both hand sewn and machine sewn snaps, hooks, eyes, and buttons were covered in LIFEPAC 4 in the mending section. However, it would be a good idea to review the material and practice the skills once again before beginning your final project.

Zippers finish the opening of a garment. Regular neckline or skirt zippers are made with metal or plastic teeth or synthetic coils. An "invisible" zipper is also available for necklines and skirts.

A sewing machine requires a special zipper foot (rather than the normal presser foot) in order to apply a zipper. Check with your machine instruction book to make sure you have the zipper foot before starting to sew your zipper. Invisible zippers also need a special zipper foot.

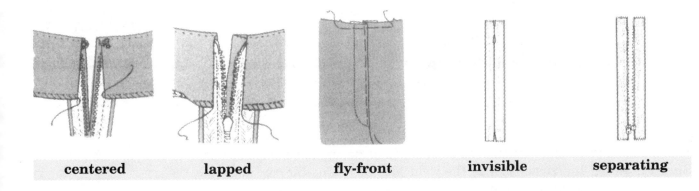

| centered | lapped | fly-front | invisible | separating |

Zippers have several basic applications. The *centered application* is a regular zipper used at the center front or back of a garment. The *lapped application* is also a regular zipper, used at the left side seam of pants, skirts, and dresses. The *fly-front application* is the traditional trouser application of a regular zipper used on pants and skirts. An invisible zipper is used for *invisible application* which can substitute for either lapped or centered. A *separating zipper* may be sewn into either a centered or lapped application, usable on jackets, vests, or skirts.

This LIFEPAC teaches the centered and fly-front methods of applying zippers. All work is done on the inside of the garment except for topstitching. Work from bottom to top of the **placket** (opening that facilitates putting on or taking off a garment) in preliminary basting and topstitching.

Centered zipper.

Step 1: Measure and mark the exact length of the placket, using the zipper as a guide. With the correct sides together, using a regular stitch length, stitch a seam from the bottom of the material up to the mark. Backstitch. Switch the machine to a basting stitch and close the remaining seam where the zipper will be placed.

Step 2: Press the seam open.

stitching

marking

basting

Step 3: Extend the right allowance and place the open zipper face down, with the top stop at the mark and the edge of the opened coil or chain along the seam line; pin in place. Using a zipper foot, machine-baste along stitching guideline on zipper tape.

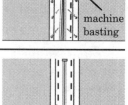

Step 4: Close the zipper, keeping the pull tab up. Extend the remaining seam allowance. Position the zipper foot to the left of the needle and machine-baste the unstitched zipper tape to the seam allowance from bottom to top, following the guideline on the tape.

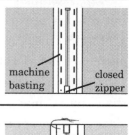

Step 5: Turn garment right side up and spread it as flat as possible. Starting at the center seam, hand baste across the bottom and side ¼" from the seam line, catching the garment, seam allowance, and zipper tape. Repeat for the other side.

Step 6: Change to a regular stitch length. Beginning at the bottom of the placket, just outside the basting, topstitch through all three layers—garment, allowance and zipper tape. Take 2 or 3 stitches across bottom of the placket, pivot, and stitch to top.

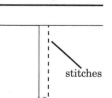

Step 7: Position the zipper foot to the right side of the needle and topstitch the remaining side in the same way, taking the same number of stitches across the bottom of the placket. Pull thread ends to the incorrect side and tie. Remove hand bastings and open the placket.

Fly-front zipper (right over left).

The fly-front zipper is the traditional zipper for men's trousers and women's sport clothes because it provides a neat and durable closing. Its placket has a definite lap direction: in women's clothes it laps right over left, but in men's garments left over right. Overall, it's best to buy a pattern with a fly-front closing, its pattern will supply all the necessary pieces. Although the fly-front zipper is somewhat complicated, it is included especially for the gentlemen who might choose to make a pair of shorts or slacks. Women, reverse the rights and lefts in the instructions so that your front flap will be in the correct direction.

Step 1: On the front right, mark the topstitching curve with hand basting; mark the bottom of the placket. Stitch the crotch from this marking down to within 1″ to 1 ½″ from the edge of the inside leg.

Step 2: With right sides together, baste the right fly facing to the right front edge, matching their markings. Stitch from the marking at the bottom of zipper placket to the waist. Remove basting.

Step 3: Trim and grade the seam allowances; open out the facing. Press the facing and the allowances away from the garment.

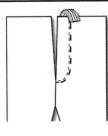

Step 4: Position the closed zipper face down on the right side of the facing. The left edge of the zipper tape should lie along the facing seam and the bottom stop should be ³/₄" from the facing's raw edge. The top of the zipper may extend beyond the upper edge of the facing. Baste the zipper in place, turning up the bottom of the left zipper tape even with the bottom stop. Baste the left zipper tape to the facing from bottom to top. On the right zipper tape, stitch close to the chain or coil, using the zipper foot and a regular stitch length; stitch a second time, close to the tape's edge.

Step 5: Turn the facing to the inside on the seam line. Press. On the outside of the garment, baste the fly facing to the front, following the original basted markings. Topstitch from the bottom to the top along the basted markings, being careful not to catch the left zipper tape in the stitching. Pull threads to the wrong side and tie. Remove all basting threads.

Note: At this point, the fly shield is separate; it will be added in Step 8.

Step 6: With right sides together, stitch the fly shield and the fly shield facing together on the unnotched edge. Trim and grade the seam; notch the curve. Turn shield to the right side and press. Finish the raw edge of the shield by trimming ³/₈" from the shield on the notched edge. Fold the facing over the shield's raw edge and stitch close to the fold.

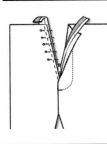

Step 7: Fold under and baste the edge of left pants front ¹/₄" beyond the seam line. Open zipper. Pin left front to right side of zipper, next to coil or chain, working from the bottom to top. Baste in place. Close zipper to check positioning.

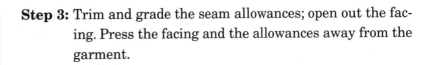

fly shield

Step 8: To position the fly shield, work from the wrong side. Match the curve of the shield to the curve of the topstitching; pin temporarily.

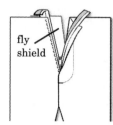

Step 9: Turn the garment back to the right side and baste through all the layers of the garment, zipper, and shield. Remove pins. Open zipper. Using a zipper foot, stitch through all layers from top to bottom, close to the coil or chain. Pull threads to the wrong side and tie.

Step 10: While zipper is still open, stitch across the zipper tapes at the waist seam line; cut off excess zipper and tapes even with the raw edge of garment. This must be done with the zipper open so the slider is not cut off. Work a bar tack by hand or machine across the seam line at the bottom of the placket, catching in the shield.

Another helpful closure is the *machine button hole*. Machine buttonholes consist of two parallel rows of zigzag stitches and two ends finished with a bar tack. It is opened only after the stitching is completed. Since each machine is different, read the instructions that come with the machine you are using to see how to make a buttonhole.

Answer the following questions.

2.52   How does a sewing machine need to be modified in order to stitch a zipper? _____

2.53   Where are you most apt to find a lapped application zipper? _____

2.54   What type of garment would you be most likely to use a separating zipper? _____

2.55   On the centered zipper, what is the only part of the work that is done on the outside of the garment?

_____

2.56   In which direction does the flap go in a man's fly-front closing? _____

_____

Complete the following activities.

2.57   Sew a *centered zipper*. Cut a 9″ x 6″ piece of fabric. Fold lengthwise and cut in half. With right sides together, sew the seam below the markings made for a 6″ zipper. Continue using the directions given in the text. Glue one edge of the fabric into your *Sewing Skills Notebook*.

Adult Check _____
                   Initial   **Date**

2.58   (Optional) Sew a *fly-front zipper* according to your pattern directions. If your chosen project pattern does not call for a fly-front zipper, then you are not required to complete this activity. If desired, you may do this activity for extra credit.

Adult Check _____
                   Initial   **Date**

2.59 Sew a *machine buttonhole*. Cut out a 5″ square piece of fabric. Fold in half. If desired, interface it for extra stability. Follow the directions given with your sewing machine. Glue the piece of fabric into your *Sewing Skills Notebook*.

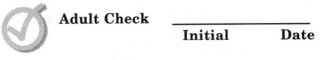

Adult Check _____

                                    Initial   **Date**

Review the material in this section in preparation for the Self Test. This Self Test will check your mastery of this particular section as well as your knowledge of the previous section.

SELF TEST 2

Matching (each answer, 3 points).

2.01 _____ hand stitch used primarily to make and repair seams

2.02 _____ used to temporarily hold together two or more fabric layers during fitting and construction

2.03 _____ is used to transfer pattern symbols

2.04 _____ machine stitch used to secure the beginning and end of a row

2.05 _____ decorative stitch done on the outside of the garment

2.06 _____ this requires a notched edge

2.07 _____ this requires a clipped edge

2.08 _____ has a self enclosed seam

2.09 _____ short, tapered, stitched area that enables the garment to fit the figure

2.010 _____ stitched folds of fabric that provide controlled fullness

2.011 _____ pulling fabric together until it is ⅓ to ½ its original width

a. backstitch

b. bar tack

c. basting

d. dart

e. even backstitch

f. flat felled

g. gathering

h. outward curved seam

i. inward curved seam

j. pleats

k. tailor tack

l. topstitch

m. tuck

Multiple choice (each answer, 3 points).

2.012 Overcasting is a small, slanting stitch placed over the raw edge of fabric to finish the edge and keep it from _____ .
    a. raveling   b. ripping
    c. snagging   d. pinking

2.013 The normal seam allowance is _____ inches unless otherwise marked.
    a. ½   b. ⅝
    c. ¾   d. ⅜

2.014 The _____ keeps material moving toward the back of the sewing machine while stitching.
    a. presser foot   b. feed dog
    c. handwheel   d. spool pin

2.015 Trimming the seam allowances within a seam to different widths is called _____ .
    a. sewing   b. cutting
    c. grading   d. raveling

2.016 The _____ regulates looseness and tightness of the stitch on a sewing machine.
    a. stitch regulator   b. tension regulator
    c. spool pin   d. bobbin

2.017 A _____ is a decorative edge finish formed by looped interlocking stitches.
    a. French stitch   b. blanket stitch
    c. blind stitch   d. dart

FAMILY AND CONSUMER SCIENCE

five

LIFEPAC TEST

80 / 100

Name _____

Date _____

Score _____

FAMILY AND CONSUMER SCIENCE 05: LIFEPAC TEST

Matching (each answer, 2 points).

1. _____ crosswise threads in the fabric
2. _____ necessary for fabrics that have more than 1% shrinkage
3. _____ lengthwise threads in the fabric
4. _____ beginners should avoid choosing these materials
5. _____ natural fiber in use for centuries; tends to shrink
6. _____ a synthetic fiber
7. _____ used to temporarily hold two pieces of fabric together
8. _____ where two pieces of material are sewn together
9. _____ used to finish raw edges at openings
10. _____ distance between the cutting line and the seam line
11. _____ folds of fabrics which control fullness and stitched to a point at one end
12. _____ a good first project for beginners
13. _____ done after each step in garment construction
14. _____ should be consulted during garment construction
15. _____ the side of the fabric that is not meant to be seen

a. basting stitch
b. cotton
c. darts
d. wrong side
e. "Easy to Make" pattern
f. facings
g. nylon
h. pattern guide sheet
i. plaids and stripes
j. preshrinking
k. pressing
l. seams
m. allowance
n. warp
o. woof

Answer *true* **or** *false* (each answer, 3 points).

16. _____ The feed dog holds the fabric in place while you stitch.
17. _____ The tension regulator is the device which regulates the looseness or tightness of the stitch.
18. _____ The selvage is the woven edge that runs parallel to the warp yarns.
19. _____ The pressure regulator controls the pull on the thread as it comes from the needle.
20. _____ The feed dog keeps the material moving along toward the back of the machine as it is being stitched.
21. _____ Patterns are available for both men and women.
22. _____ Small, irregular checks do not have to be matched.

Multiple Choice (each answer, 3 points).

23. A _____ is the diagonal line formed when woven fabric is folded so that the selvage is parallel to the crosswise thread.
    a. nap
    b. bias
    c. grain
    d. welt

24. _____ is fabric with a raised surface, like corduroy or velvet.
    a. Nap
    b. Bias
    c. Grain
    d. Welt

25. A _____ is a decorative edge finish formed by looping interlocking stitches.
    a. French stitch
    b. blanket stitch
    c. blind stitch
    d. catch stitch

26. _____ are the yarns that are interlaced at right angles to the warp yarns to produce fabrics.
    a. Fillings
    b. Fibers
    c. Facings
    d. Rick rack

27. _____ is a third layer of fabric used for shaping the garment.
    a. Lining
    b. Interlining
    c. Interfacing

28. Cutting all the seam allowances within a seam to different widths to eliminate bulk is _____ .
    a. basting
    b. grading
    c. tailoring

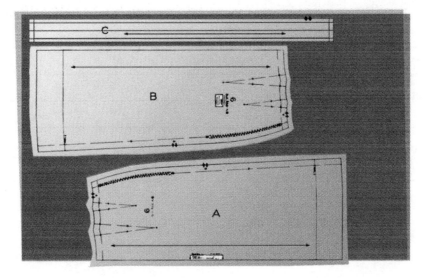

Study the layout above and answer the questions (each answer, 4 points).

29. Does the fabric have a lengthwise or a crosswise fold? _____

30. How many pieces of fabric will you have when A is cut out?_____

31. If this pattern layout is used will all of the pieces be cut on grain? _____

    Why? _____

    _____

Matching (each answer, 2 points).

a.

b.

c.

d.

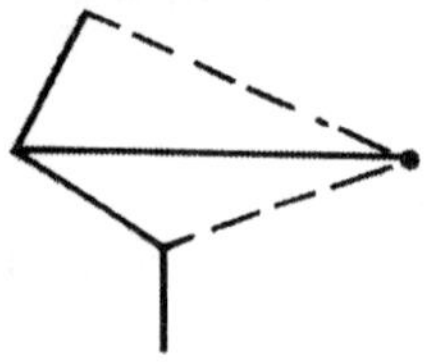

e.

f.

32. _____ straight grain of fabric

33. _____ fold of fabric

34. _____ dart

35. _____ notch

36. _____ seam line

Short Answer (each answer, 3 points).

37. According to the garment checklist in the back of the LIFEPAC, how do you lengthen a pattern piece?

   _____

   _____

38. Name two standards for a good hem. _____

   _____

39. What is a guide sheet? _____

   _____

2.018 _____ is the best seam finish for knit materials.
   a. zigzag   b. pinked
   c. self enclosed   d. French stitch

2.019 The _____ is the metal plate directly under the needle on the sewing machine.
   a. throat plate   b. bobbin
   c. bobbin case   d. feed dog

2.020 A _____ is the spool which holds the lower thread used in stitching.
   a. spool pin   b. bobbin
   c. needle bar   d. shuttle

2.021 A facing is the fabric used to finish raw edges of a garment at the _____ .
   a. neckline   b. waist
   c. hem   d. pleat

2.022 A _____ zipper application is most often used in men's trousers.
   a. centered   b. lapped
   c. fly-front

Short Answers (each answer, 6 points).

2.023 Which thread is pulled in gathering? _____

2.024 How does a sewing machine need to be modified before stitching a zipper? _____

_____

2.025 How do you reinforce the ends of a dart? _____

Essay (answer, 16 points).

2.026 Explain the steps in hemming a garment. Include the measurements and how you figure them.

_____

_____

_____

_____

_____

_____

_____

_____

_____

_____

Score _____

Adult Check _____

III. SELECTING PATTERN, FABRIC, AND NOTIONS

Patterns and designs are available in order to make clothes, purses, hats, toys, and home accessories. You must understand all of the information located on the pattern envelope, guide sheet, and the markings themselves in order to correctly construct the garment.

It takes skill to choose a pattern that both becomes you and is easily constructed. It takes artistry to turn fabric and notions into a garment perfectly constructed to you.

SECTION OBJECTIVES

Review these objectives. When you have completed this section, you should be able to:

5. Select a pattern that is the correct in size and style to flatter your figure.

6. Select fabric and notions appropriate for your pattern.

7. Interpret the pattern envelope, guide sheet, and pattern symbols.

8. Understand layout and fabric cutting.

9. Use a tracing wheel and tracing paper to transfer pattern markings from the pattern to the fabric.

10. Correctly press seams and darts.

FIT

To successfully create a garment, you must start with the correct pattern size. Patterns are sized for different measurements, proportions and heights. Study figure types and compare measurements regularly.

Women. Wearing underwear or a body suit, take your measurements and then appraise your front and side silhouette in a long mirror.

Measurements. When measuring across, be sure to measure parallel to the floor.

1. *Height.* Shoeless, stand with your back flat against a wall, holding a ruler atop your head parallel to the floor. Hold the ruler in place and walk away. Measure your height from the floor to the ruler's mark on the wall.

2. *High bust.* With a tape measure, measure directly under the arm above the full bustline and straight across the back. (NOTE: high bust measurement is not always listed with other pattern body measurements. However, when there is a difference of 2″ or more between high and full bust measurements, high bust is a truer indicator of appropriate garment size.)

3. *Bust/chest.* The fullest part of the bust, high under the arm and straight across the back.

4. *Waist.* Natural waistline (indentation).

5. *Hip.* The fullest part, 7-9 inches below the natural waistline.

6. *Back waist.* The top of the most prominent bone at the base of the neck to the natural waistline.

7. *Center front waist.* The neckline seam to natural waistline.

8. *Sleeve length.* Shoulder to wrist with elbow slightly bent.

9. *Sleeve width.* Around the fullest part of upper arm.

10. *Thigh width.* Around the fullest part of upper thigh.

11. *Crotch.* (seated) Natural waistline to chair seat, plus ½ to 1″ ease.
12. *Pants length.* Side of leg from natural waistline to ankle bone or as desired. Allow for hem.
13. *Skirt length.* Natural waistline in center front to desired length. Allow for hem.

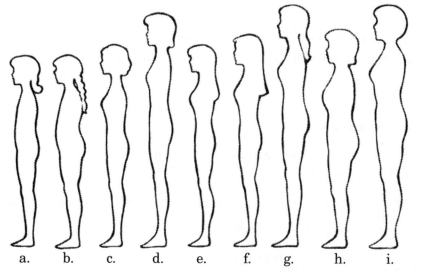

	Figure Type	Height	Description
a.	Girl	from 4 2″ to 5 1″	The smallest. For short girls who have not started to physically mature, requiring few darts for figure contours.
b.	Girls Plus	from 4 2″ to 5 1″	The growing girl who weighs more than the average for her age and height. Girl and girls plus patterns are the same height in comparable sizes.
c.	Young Junior/Teen	about 5 1″ to 5 3″	Tall girls just beginning to develop in the bust and hips.
d.	Junior	about 5 4″ to 5 5″	The well-developed figure with a shorter waist length than the Misses.
e.	Junior Petite	about 5 to 5 1″	Well developed, with a smaller body build and shorter waist length than the Junior.
f.	Miss Petite	about 5 2″ to 5 4″	Well developed, but shorter than average from the shoulder to the waistline.
g.	Miss	about 5 5″ to 5 8″	Medium-tall, with well-proportioned figure; the "average" figure.
h.	Half-size	about 5 2″ to 5 3″	Fully developed, short waisted, thick in the waist and hip.
i.	Woman	about 5 5″ to 5 6″	Larger, more mature, about the same height as a Miss.

Each pattern type is made in a range of sizes, such as 10, 12, 14, and 16. As opposed to other patterns, junior petites' sizes are indicated with odd numbers, such as 7, 9, 11, and 13. Young Junior/Teens sizes are marked 5/6, 7/8, etc.

33

Choosing a pattern.

1. Dress, blouse, coat, or jacket sizes are selected according to full bust measurements.

2. Skirt or pants sizes are determined by hip measurement, even if they are proportionately larger than the waist.

3. If your measurements do not exactly correspond to any one size, consider all pertinent factors and choose the size requiring the least amount of adjustment.

Men.

Measurements.

1. *Height.* (see women's)

2. *Shoulder.* From neck base (shrug shoulders to locate it) to top of the arm (raise arm shoulder high to locate the joint).

3. *Sleeve length.* From neck base at center back, along shoulder, over slightly bent arm to the wrist.

4. *Neckband.* Around neck at Adam's apple plus additional ½″.

5. *Arm length.* From top of arm, over bent elbow, to wrist bone.

6. *Chest.* Around the fullest part.

7. *Waist.* While wearing pants, measuring around where the waist seam rests.

8. *Hips (seat).* Around the fullest part.

9. *Trouser inseam.* Inside of leg to the hem (or desired length).

10. *Trouser outseam.* The outside side seam from waistline to hem (for desired length).

The Three Body Types

Boys. A young growing person.

Teen boys. A youth who has not yet attained adult proportions.

Men. A mature physique and average height of 5 10″

To determine the correct pattern size, compare the measurements you have taken to the **size range chart**. Select a jacket or coat size according to the chest measurement, a shirt by the neckband, and trousers according to the waist. If measurements fall between two sizes, buy the larger size for a husky build, the smaller size for one that is slender. When pattern types are grouped together (for example, shirt plus trousers), choose the size according to the chest measurement and adjust the trousers if necessary.

Answer *true* **or** *false*.

3.1 _____ Understanding figure types will help you determine your pattern size.

3.2 _____ Figure types describe age groups.

3.3 _____ Accurate measurements are essential to a well-fitting garment.

3.4 _____ Sleeve length is measured from the neck base to the wrist with the elbow bent slightly.

3.5 _____ The neckband is measured around the neck at the Adam's apple plus 1″.

3.6 _____ Young Junior/Teen pattern sizes are marked 7, 9, and 11.

Complete these statements.

3.7 Women measure their waist at _____ .

3.8 Hip measurements are made _____ .

3.9 Sleeve width is measured _____ .

3.10 Height is measured _____ .

3.11 Back waist length is measured from _____ .

3.12 Trouser inseam is measured along _____ .

3.13 In selecting a pattern for a lady's blouse, select the size which best fits your _____ .

3.14 When selecting a pattern for a man's shirt, select the size which best fits your _____ .

Complete this activity.

3.15 Choose a partner and measure each other. Record all you measurements and determine you figure type and size.

Girls chart:

Date: _____   Height: _____   Weight: _____

	Your Measurements:	Pattern Measurements:	Difference Plus Minus
High bust			
Bust			
Waist			
Hip			
Back waist			
Center front waist			
Sleeve length			
Sleeve width			
Thigh width			
Crotch			
Pants length			
Skirt length			

Boys chart:

Date: _____ Height: _____ Weight: _____

	Your Measurements:	Pattern Measurements:	Difference Plus Minus
Chest			
Waist			
Hip (seat)			
Neckband			
Sleeve length			
Shoulder			
Arm length			
Trouser outseam			
Trouser inseam			

My measurements are closest to a _____ figure type, size _____ .

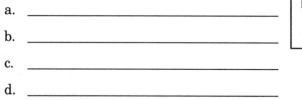 **Adult Check** _____

                                                  Initial   **Date**

THE LANGUAGE OF PATTERNS

Envelope. The front of the pattern's envelope has several images of what the completed garment should look like. Select the one you wish to make. These also give you suggestions on suitable materials for the garment. Near the top, it will list the pattern company, number, the price, and the size. Patterns are not returnable. Read the envelope carefully, making sure that you have the proper size before buying it.*

McCall's pattern #7546

 **Complete this list.**

3.16 List four pieces of information found on the front of a pattern envelope.

a. _____

b. _____

c. _____

d. _____

*The pattern references in this Lifepac are from McCall's pattern #7546.

36

Perhaps the most important part of understanding the envelope back is determining the amount of material to buy. The yardage will be based on the end result you chose, the garment's size, the fabric's width, and its nap (if you use **napped fabric**). The yardage chart also gives fabric amounts for lining, interfacing and trims.

Reading the pattern envelope before purchasing the fabric itself very important. On the envelope back, you will see the same general information:

1. Pattern number
2. Number of pieces (the fewer the pieces, the easier it is to make)
3. Pictures of pattern pieces (optional, not all patterns show this on the back)
4. Back views of pattern styles
5. Garment description
6. Suggested fabric
7. Notions needed
8. Finished garment measurements
9. Information on special fabrics (uses or suitability of plaids, stripes, diagonals, or napped fabrics)
10. Standard body measurements (also given in metrics)
11. Yardage chart

7546 **MISSES' DRESS IN TWO LENGTHS:** Loose fitting pullover dress with long or short sleeves has raised waist seam and full gathered skirt; dress A with fabric mixing and dress B feature front patch pockets; dress C has center front slit revealing a contrasting underlay; dress D features scalloped lace sleeves and lace overskirt.

BODY MEASUREMENTS										
Size	10	12	14	16	18	20	22	24	26	
Bust	32½	34	36	38	40	42	44	46	48	Ins.
Waist	25	26½	28	30	32	34	37	39	41	"
Hip	34½	36	38	40	42	44	46	48	50	"
Back waist length	16	16¼	16½	16¾	17	17¼	17½	17¾	18	"

Combinations: C(10-12-14), D(12-14-16), E(14-16-18), G(20-22-24). GW(22-24-26)

SIZES	10	12	14	16	18	20	22	24	26	
VIEW A - Dress										
Color 1 (Front and Back Bodice)										
44/45" ***	1	1	1	1	1⅛	1⅛	1⅛	1⅛	1⅛	Yds.
58/60" ***	¾	¾	¾	¾	¾	¾	¾	¾	⅞	Yd.
Color 2 (Sleeves and Pockets)										
44/45" ***	⅞	⅞	⅞	1⅛	1⅛	1⅛	1¼	1¼	1⅜	Yds.
58/60" ***	¾	¾	¾	⅞	⅞	⅞	⅞	⅞	⅞	Yd.
Color 3 (Skirt)										
44" thru 60" ***	2¼	2¼	2¼	2¼	2¼	2¼	2¼	2¼	2¼	Yds.
Interfacing - 21" thru 25", ½ yd.										
VIEW B - Dress										
44/45" **	2¾	2¾	2¾	2⅞	2⅞	2⅞	3	3	3	Yds.
58/60" **	2½	2½	2½	2½	2⅝	2⅝	2⅝	2⅝	2⅝	"
Interfacing - 21" thru 25", ½ yd.										
VIEW C - Dress										
44/45" **	3¼	3⅜	3¾	4	4¼	4¼	4⅜	4⅜	4⅜	Yds.
58/60" **	2⅞	2⅞	2⅞	3	3⅛	3⅛	3¼	3¼	3¼	"
Contrast Underlay										
44" thru 60" **	1⅛	1⅛	1⅛	1⅛	1⅛	1⅛	1⅛	1⅛	1⅛	"
Interfacing - 21" thru 25", ½ yd.										
VIEW D - Dress										
44/45" **	2⅜	2⅜	2½	2½	2½	2½	2⅝	2¾	2¾	Yds.
58/60" **	2	2	2	2	2	2	2	2	2	"
Sleeves and Overskirt										
45" Lace	2¼	2¼	2¼	2⅜	2⅜	2⅜	2½	2½	2½	"
52/54" Lace	1½	1⅝	1⅝	1⅝	1⅝	1¾	1¾	1¾	1⅞	"
Interfacing - 21" thru 25", ½ yd.										
FINISHED GARMENT MEASUREMENTS										
Back length from normal neckline										
Dress A, C	50¼	50½	50¾	51	51¼	51½	51¾	52	52¼	Ins.
Dress B, D	37¼	37½	37¾	38	38¼	38½	38¾	39	39¼	"
Measurement at bustline										
Dress A thru D	37	38½	40½	42½	44½	46½	48½	50½	52½	"
Bottom width										
Dress A thru D	72	73½	75	76½	78	79½	81	82½	84	"

****Without Nap *****With or Without Nap** - Use With Nap Yardages and layouts for pile or one-way design fabrics. Additional Fabric may be needed to match stripes or plaids.

SUGGESTED FABRICS: Dress A thru D - Rayon Blends • Cotton Blends • Lightweight Linen • Challis; **Dress A, B, C** - also Gingham • Seersucker • Gauze • Allover Eyelet; **Sleeves and Overskirt D** - Double-edge Scalloped Lace. **NOTE: All Garments** - Not Suitable For Diagonals.

NOTIONS: Thread; **Dress B** - 1½ Yds. of ¼" Wide Cording (Opt.).

11 PATTERN PIECES

Complete the following activities using the sample pattern envelope. (Although the following activities are completed with the use of a dress pattern, the principles are the same for the men. All are required to do the work.)

3.17 Study the picture the an envelope back to the right. Using the list above, label the information.

3.18 Jill is going to make View B. Her fabric is 44″/45″ wide (115 cm) without nap. She is Size 12.

a. Circle the view.

b. Circle the size.

c. Circle the width of fabric—without nap.

d. Draw a line across from the fabric width and a line down from her size.

e. Where the two lines cross is the yardage of the fabric needed.

f. How many yards of fabric should Jill buy?

____

Adult Check ____________
Initial **Date**

Answer the following questions using the preceding envelope back.

3.19   How many views are available with this pattern? _____

3.20   Name five fabrics from which View A could be made.

　　　　a. _____   d. _____

　　　　b. _____   e. _____

　　　　c. _____

3.21   How many yards of cording is needed for View B? _____

3.22   What size dress would be correct for 36 inch bust? _____

3.23   How much fabric is needed for View C dress in Size 12 with 45″ fabric? _____

3.24   How much lace is needed for View D sleeves and overskirt in Size 12 with 45″ lace? _____

3.25   How much interfacing is need for View A, B, C, or D, Size 12? _____

Contents. All pattern envelopes contain the same basic information. The key element is the *tissue pattern* with each piece identified by name, number, and view (when applicable). Most pieces represent half a garment section and are placed on the fabric fold, because garments are usually identical on their right and left sides.

The other item found in the envelope is the *guide sheet*. It should be studied carefully before doing anything else. The guide sheet consists of the name and number of the pattern, piece diagram, cutting guides, alteration instructions, pattern markings, cutting and marking instructions, and step-by-step sewing instructions.

The numbers indicating the front and back views of the pattern are necessary to be assured that you are using the correct guide sheet for your project and can see clearly what the garment will look like both front and back. The piece diagram is useful for identifying what pieces are needed for each view.

Pattern Storage

Trying to put pattern pieces back into the envelope once they are out is like putting toothpaste back into the tube. Instead, tape a gallon-size zippered plastic freezer bag to your sewing machine. Put the pattern envelope, extra pattern pieces, and the guide sheet into this bag—it is much easier than using the pattern envelope, and everything fits.

Then, when you finish with each pattern piece, fold it so the pattern number, name, and company name shows. This way, if you forget to mark something, you can see it through the freezer bag and locate it easily without unfolding and shuffling through multiple pieces.[1]

The *pattern markings* or symbols tell you how to sew the pattern pieces together. Each piece is marked with a style number, size, identification number, view letter, and name (front, back, side). Center back and center front are marked as is the natural waistline. The pattern piece also tells you how many pieces to cut out. Most pieces have alteration guidelines as well.

1. Saunders, Jan, *Sewing for Dummies*, IDG Books Worldwide, Inc., Foster City, CA p.46

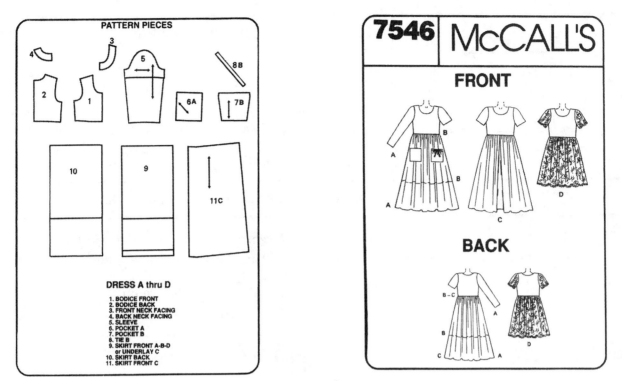

Two portions of a guide sheet.

Construction markings or symbols help you read the pattern. Some patterns have many markings and others have only a few.

Construction Markings.

•	<u>Dots</u> used to match seams and other construction details.
— — — — — — —	<u>Seam line</u> (aka stitching line) a broken line.
▬▬▬▬▬▬▬	<u>Cutting line</u> a heavy, solid line.
— — — — — — ▬▬▬▬▬▬▬	<u>Seam allowance</u> distance between the seam line and cutting line, typically $^5/_8''$.
◆◆ 1　　2 ◆ ✂	<u>Notches</u> along seam line aid in joining pieces together. Each is numbered and the corresponding numbers are joined together when sewing. Should be cut out, away from the seam line. Two or more should be cut as one large notch.
— — ▶ — —	<u>Arrows</u> on seam lines indicate the direction you should stitch. Stitching the wrong way will distort the fabric grain.
◀——————▶	<u>Grain-line arrow</u> the pattern piece should be placed on the fabric with the grain-line arrow parallel to the lengthwise grain.
▼————————▼	<u>Fold-line arrow</u> the edge of the pattern should be placed exactly along the lengthwise fold of the fabric.

(diagram of dart)	<u>Darts</u> a solid line for folding and two broken lines for stitching.
(diagram of alteration lines)	<u>Alteration lines</u> Two solid lines close together. The pattern is folded to shorten. To lengthen, cut between the lines and separate evenly.
(diagram of buttonhole)	<u>Buttonhole</u> marks the place for buttonholes.

The cutting guides give recommended layouts for different views, several fabric widths, and the pattern's entire size range. The illustrations below show the cutting layout for Views A and B, all sizes.

Key:

⬛ fabric

▢ printed side of pattern up

▨ printed side of pattern down

A DRESS

Color 1 (Front and Back Bodice)
use pieces 1 thru 4

44" 45" (115cm)
fabric
with nap or
without nap
all sizes

58" 60" (150cm)
fabric
with nap or
without nap
all sizes

Color 2 (Sleeves and Pockets)
use pieces 5, 6

44" thru 60"
(115cm thru 150cm)
fabric
with nap or
without nap
all sizes

Color 3 (Skirt)
use pieces 9, 10

44" thru 60"
(115cm thru 150cm)
fabric
with nap or
without nap
all sizes

B DRESS
use pieces 1 thru 5; 7, 8, 9, 10

44" 45" (115cm)
fabric
without nap
all sizes

58" 60" (150cm)
fabric
without nap
all sizes

Interfacing
use pieces 3, 4

21" thru 25"
(53cm thru 64cm)
all sizes

Step-by-step sewing instructions for constructing garment parts in their proper order are given with sketches that illustrate the technique. Read through the entire set of sewing instructions before beginning in order to give yourself an overview of what to expect. Take each step as it comes and follow the directions precisely in order to avoid discouragement and confusion.

Answer the following questions about the guide sheet.

3.26 What pattern pieces are needed for each color of View A?

Color 1: _____ Color 2: _____ Color 3: _____

3.27 What pattern pieces are needed for View B? _____

3.28 What pattern pieces are needed for interfacing? _____

3.29 Which pattern piece(s) for View B is/are not placed on the fold of the fabric? _____

Match these symbols.

3.30 _____ ■   a. printed side of pattern down

3.31 _____ □   b. fabric

3.32 _____ ▨   c. printed side of pattern up

Answer *true* **or** *false*.

3.33 _____ Dress piece 2 is placed face down on View A, 50″/60″ fabric.

3.34 _____ Dress piece 5 is never placed on the lengthwise fold.

3.35 _____ View B has more pattern pieces than View A.

3.36 _____ Dress piece 9 is always placed on the crosswise fold.

Complete the following activity.

3.37 Write the term that identifies the symbol for each letter on the diagram.

a. _____

b. _____

c. _____

d. _____

e. _____

f. _____

g. _____

h. _____

i. _____

j. _____

k. _____

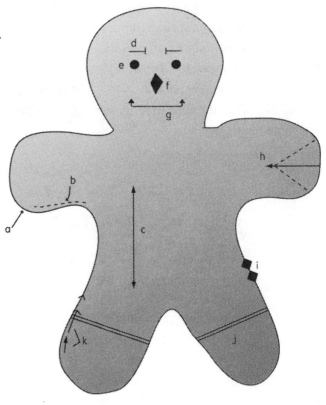

41

PATTERN

Patterns are available for both beginning sewers and experienced seamstresses. For your first project, choose one that will challenge your ability yet will not be so difficult that you will get frustrated and never want to sew again. The fewer the pieces, the easier it is to sew. Those labeled "easy to sew" or "jiffy" can occasionally be misleading. Look on the back of the envelope to see how many pieces are in the pattern.

Choose a pattern in a style you like, one that looks good on you and in your size. It should require many of the construction processes that you have already learned. Some suggested projects are a gathered skirt with a casing or waistband; an A-line or straight skirt; pair of slacks with front-fly zipper (more challenging); gathered jogging pants with casing or waistband; a simple dress or top; a shirt; or a bathrobe.

> **Note.** The knowledge gained in the construction of garments will also be invaluable for tailoring and mending clothes.

Complete the following activities.

3.38   A pattern with _____ pieces will be easiest to sew.

3.39   Some patterns that are labeled "easy to sew" or " _____ ," are occasionally misleading.

3.40   Choose a pattern in a style you like, one that looks good on you and one in your _____ .

FABRIC

As a beginner, you need to select fabric that is easy to handle. You need to master both the sewing machine and stitching a straight seam before you select a more hard-to-handle material.

Sheer and shiny fabrics tend to slip and slide under the presser foot, and stitches are difficult to remove from them. Bulky fabrics are hard to cut accurately. Single knits can also be difficult because the edges roll and the seams stretch. Choose a firmly woven fabric like kettlecloth, gingham, broadcloth, or (if it suits your pattern) a polyester knit blend. The back of the envelope makes fabric suggestions for the pattern.

Fabrics are manufactured in solid colors, plaids, stripes, or designs. Fabrics can have an all-over or a **one-way design.**

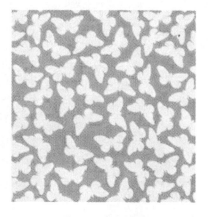

All-over design

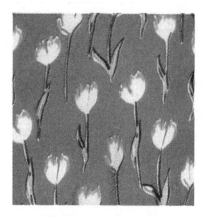

One way design

Fabrics with an all-over design need no special attention, but one-way designed fabrics require extra fabric in order to lay all the pattern pieces in one direction before cutting.

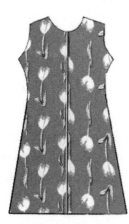

Incorrect

Correct

Fabrics with large stripes, plaids, or certain prints also require the purchase of extra fabric for matching the designs. You will need to lay out the pattern pieces on the fabric in such a way so the plaids, stripes, or prints match at the seam. Using notches is helpful in proper layout for matching designs.

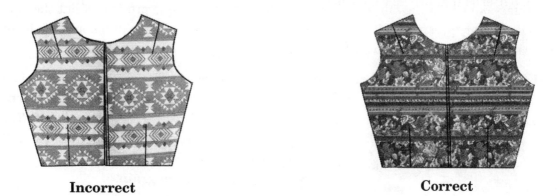

Incorrect   **Correct**

Small prints, stripes, or checks do not necessarily have to be matched, but you may choose to do so. For your first project, select a solid fabric or one that will not have to be matched.

Compare prices when shopping. Buy a medium-priced fabric as a beginner, but avoid cheap, poorly made material which often stretches out of shape while sewing. Read the ends of the fabric bolts for fiber and care information. Consider this information when choosing a fabric to sew.

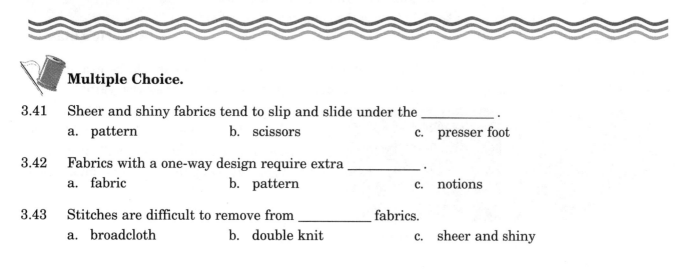

Multiple Choice.

3.41   Sheer and shiny fabrics tend to slip and slide under the _____ .
         a. pattern   b. scissors   c. presser foot

3.42   Fabrics with a one-way design require extra _____ .
         a. fabric   b. pattern   c. notions

3.43   Stitches are difficult to remove from _____ fabrics.
         a. broadcloth   b. double knit   c. sheer and shiny

3.44   A beginning sewer should buy _____ material.
   a. cheap   b. medium-priced   c. expensive

FABRIC PREPARATION

After purchasing your material, prepare it for use. Two preparations are preshrinking and straightening.

Preshrinking. From your study of fibers in *Family and Consumer Science 4*, you will remember that some fibers shrink. Cotton, wool, linen, and rayon are notable for shrinkage. Many fabrics have been treated so that a minimal amount or no shrinkage occurs. Read the end of the bolt of fabric to find out if the fabric will shrink or not. **Preshrink** (or material before using) material that has more than 1% shrinkage listed on the bolt.

Preshrinking a fabric involves laundering and drying it just as you will do after the garment is made. If your family typically washes clothes in hot water and dries everything in the clothes dryer on medium heat, use that same process to preshrink the material. Either fill a sink with hot water and soak the material for several minutes or wash it in the washing machine on the hot setting. Preshrink any trim or zippers in the same manner as the fabric. Sometimes when the material is preshrunk but the zipper is not, the zipper will appear "puckered" after the first washing because of the small amount of shrinkage. The same thing can occur with trims as well.

Straightening. Grain is the direction of the crosswise and lengthwise yarns or threads of a fabric. All woven fabrics are made of lengthwise threads (or **warp**), through which are interlaced the crosswise threads (or **woof**). The **selvage** is the woven edge that runs parallel to the warp yarns. The fabric has two selvages–one on each side. Crosswise woof is called **filling grain**. Filling grains go across the fabric from one selvage to its opposite. The **raw edge** is the one where the fabric is cut. The lengthwise fabric edges, those without selvages, are raw edges.

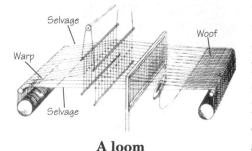

A loom

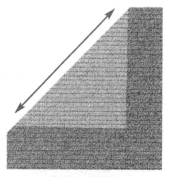

A fabric's bias

Imagine a line lies diagonally across the lengthwise yarns and the crosswise yarns. The diagonal line is the **bias**. The bias grain has the most stretch in a woven fabric. It is formed when the lengthwise thread is folded parallel to the crosswise thread.

During milling, the fabric is often pulled out of shape. Therefore, the grain should be examined. In **grain perfect** fabrics, the lengthwise yarns are at a ninety-degree angle to the crosswise yarns.

Grain-perfect fabric is necessary for a well fitting garment. If the fabric is off-grain or if the pattern is cut off-grain, the garment will drape incorrectly. Also, they will pull and be uncomfortable to wear.

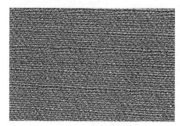

Off-grain fabric

Grain perfect fabric

Grain perfect

Off-grain

Grain perfect.

1. Raw or torn edges meet
2. Selvages meet
3. Flat fold

Off grain.

1. Raw edges do not meet,
2. Selvages do not meet
3. Fold ripples, doesn't lie flat.

When checking the grain line of your fabric, the raw edge must follow a crosswise thread exactly. If it does not, tear a small amount of the fabric from selvage to selvage, or pull one crosswise thread starting at the shorter side, and then cut.

You can straighten fabric by pulling on the diagonal grain of the material. A partner can help you by each taking a diagonal corner and tugging. The pulling will help bring the woof perpendicular to the selvage.

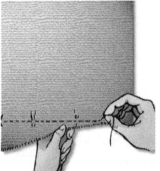

Pulling thread to check grain.

Clipping along a crosswise thread.

Define these terms.

3.45   preshrink   _____

3.46   selvage   _____

3.47   grain perfect   _____

Answer the following.

3.48   Should you preshrink trim and zippers?   _____

3.49   The lengthwise threads of woven fabrics is also known as the _____ .

3.50   The crosswise threads of woven fabrics is also known as the _____ .

3.51   What are you trying to do when you pull the diagonal grain of fabric?

_____

_____

3.52 What three characteristics do grain perfect fabrics have?

a. _____

b. _____

c. _____

NOTIONS

Notions are extra supplies needed to complete a garment. The notions needed to complete your garment are listed on the back of the pattern envelope. Choose a *thread* one shade darker than and of similar fiber content to your fabric. Select a *zipper* in the size your pattern calls for and a color that matches your fabric.

rickrack

Rickrack trim on a dress.

Buttons may be used to accent your garment, even if the pattern does not require them. If you choose to make a skirt with a casing, you will need to buy "non-roll" elastic in the width called for on your pattern.

Interfacing (or a third layer of fabric used for shaping) is used at the neckline or skirt waistband and should be similar in weight to your fabric. Non-woven interfacing is a good choice for the beginner because it has no grain and can be cut in any direction. Some non-woven interfacing is fusible, being ironed rather than basted to the fabric. Non-woven does not ravel when laundered. Choose an interfacing that matches the care instructions and shrinkage percentage of your fabric.

Trimming. Rickrack, woven braid, and ribbon are easy to apply. Even if your pattern doesn't call for them, you can use your imagination.

Before leaving the store, be sure you have all the necessary material and notions. Buying them together saves time and helps in accurately matching colors.

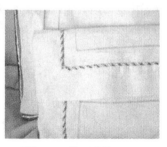

Woven braid on a towel.

Complete this list.

3.53 List five notions that may be needed to complete your garment.

a. _____

b. _____

c. _____

d. _____

e. _____

Review the material in this section in preparation for the Self Test. This Self Test will check your mastery of this particular section as well as your knowledge of all previous sections.

SELF TEST 3

Multiple Choice (each answer, 3 points).

3.01 The most common amount of a seam allowance is _____ inches.
  a. $\frac{1}{4}$ b. $\frac{5}{8}$
  c. $\frac{3}{8}$ d. $\frac{1}{2}$

3.02 _____ is the machine stitch which forms over the raw edge of the fabric in order to avoid raveling.
  a. Basting b. Backstitching
  c. Under-stitching d. Overcast

3.03 A fabric to use that would not require an additional amount of fabric to be bought would be one with a _____ .
  a. one-way design b. nap
  c. small print d. bold plaid

3.04 The grain line with the most stretch is the _____ .
  a. bias b. crosswise
  c. selvage d. lengthwise

3.05 A pattern with _____ pieces will be the easiest to sew.
  a. 5 b. 7
  c. 10 d. 12

3.06 Fabric should be preshrunk if its shrinkage percentage rate is more than _____ percent.
  a. 2 b. 3
  c. 10 d. 1

3.07 The direction of the lengthwise threads and the crosswise threads in the fabric is the _____ .
  a. nap b. warp
  c. grain d. woof

3.08 The yarns that are interlaced at right angles to the warp yarns to produce fabrics are _____ .
  a. fibers b. facings
  c. fillings d. napped

3.09 _____ is a suitable fabric used to give shape to the garment.
  a. Lining b. Interfacing
  c. Interlining d. Rickrack

Complete the following sentences (each answer, 4 points).

3.010 To make a plain seam, place the _____ sides of the fabric together.

3.011 To stitch temporarily by machine or by hand is called _____ .

3.012 Extra sewing supplies needed to complete a garment are called _____ .

3.013 Accurate_____ are essential to a well-fitting garment.

3.014 The distance between the cutting line and the seam line is called the _____ .

3.015 The _____ is used to start and stop the sewing machine.

Matching. Write the letter found on the diagram next to the term that identifies it (each answer, 3 points).

3.016 _____ grain line arrow

3.017 _____ seam line

3.018 _____ dart

3.019 _____ notch

3.020 _____ cutting line

3.021 _____ alteration line

Listing (each answer, 3 points).

3.022 List three things found on the back of a pattern envelope.

a. _____

b. _____

c. _____

3.023 List two things found on the front of the pattern envelope.

a. _____

b. _____

3.024 List four things found on the pattern guide sheet.

a. _____

b. _____

c. _____

d. _____

B

D

Bodice Front

A

F

E

C

77 / 96

Score _____

Adult Check _____

Initial   Date

48

IV. LAYOUT, CUTTING, MARKING, AND PRESSING

Once the pattern, fabric, and notions are selected, the real preparation begins. Instructions for laying the pattern on the fabric are found on the guide sheet. When the layout instructions are satisfactorily completed, you are ready to cut the fabric. Transfer *all* construction symbols before removing pattern pieces from the fabric.

SECTION OBJECTIVES

Review these objectives. When you have completed this section, you should be able to:

8. Understand the layout and cutting of fabric.
9. Use a tracing wheel and tracing paper to transfer pattern markings from the pattern to the fabric.
10. Correctly press seams and darts.

LAYOUT

Remove the guide sheet from the pattern envelope. Find the layout for your pattern by checking the view number, size, and width of the fabric. Refer to the layouts shown previously.

Study the layout carefully. Following the diagram, fold the fabric. It will need either a lengthwise or crosswise fold. The fold must always be on grain, running parallel to the opposite thread.

Pattern layout.

1. Fold fabric according to the guide-sheet diagram.
2. Press pattern pieces with a warm, dry iron.
3. Without pinning, place all the pattern pieces on the fabric according to the diagram.
4. Pin the pieces that belong on the fold (marked with a ▼ ▼) first. Place the edges of the pattern pieces exactly on the fold of the fabric. Place pins every six to eight inches at right angles to the fold.
5. Pieces with a grain line arrow ◄————► must be placed exactly on the grain. Pin only the ends of the arrow at first. Measure first from one end of the arrow to the selvage and then from the other end of the arrow to the selvage. The measurements have to be exactly the same in order for the pattern to be on grain.
6. Make sure the pattern pieces are not overlapping.
7. Smooth out the pattern pieces from the pinned fold lines or grain lines and put pins diagonally into the corners. Pinpoints should touch the cutting edge of the pattern pieces.
8. Pin the sides of the pattern next. Place pins at right angles to the cutting edge, with points toward the cutting line.
9. Do not let the pinpoints extend past the cutting line.
10. Put a pin in each notch. The pin will keep you from accidentally cutting off the notch.

Complete this activity.

4.1 Find as many errors as you can on the pattern layout below. List them and tell how each error can be corrected.

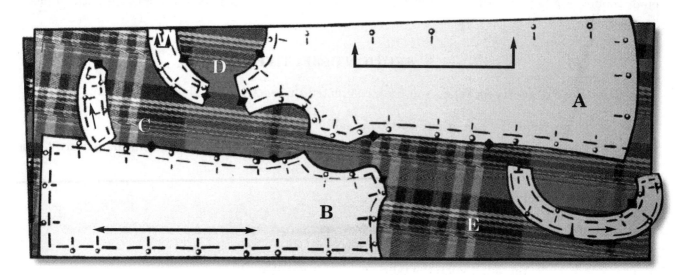

a. _____

b. _____

c. _____

d. _____

e. _____

f. _____

g. _____

h. _____

i. _____

CUTTING

When the layout is correct, the fabric is ready to cut. Cut as straight and even with the cutting line as possible. Accuracy is vital.

1. Use dressmaker's shears. Cutting with any other type can result in inaccuracies.

2. Use long, firm strokes for long edges. Use shorter strokes for curves.

3. Cut exactly on the cutting line ————— with the pattern pieces always to your left.

4. Keep the fabric flat by placing your hand on the pattern and fabric alongside of where you are cutting.

50

5. Move the fabric as little as possible. Walk around the table to cut rather than turning the fabric and pattern.

6. Cut notches away from (not towards) the seam allowance. Cut multiple notches as one large notch.

6.

7. Slash and clip lines will be cut later when sewing the garment.

8. Do not cut on the fold lines.

4.

Answer *true* or *false.*

4.2 _____ You can use any shears you wish to cut out a pattern, as long as they are sharp.

4.3 _____ You must keep the fabric as flat as possible.

4.4 _____ Cut multiple notches as one large notch.

4.5 _____ Places marked "CLIP" on the pattern pieces should be clipped while you are cutting out the pattern.

MARKING

Marking is the transferring of construction symbols (those that give directions for sewing) from the pattern to the wrong side of the fabric. Darts, dots, button holes, and placement lines for pockets and trims should all be marked.

Mark the fabric with *tailor's tacks* and *tailor's chalk. Felt-tip pens* for marking the placement of trims, hems and alterations are available in two types. One type leaves a mark that fades and disappears within a few hours, the other rinses out with water. The most efficient marking method is the use of a **tracing wheel** and **tracing paper**. It is convenient because you can mark back-pieces of fabric at the same time.

a tracing wheel

Use dressmaker's tracing paper on light- to medium-weight fabric, for it is not appropriate for sheer or bulky fabrics.

Marking with a tracing wheel and paper.

1. Choose a color tracing paper that will show on your fabric. Use a light color on light-colored fabric. Test the tracing paper on a scrap of fabric to be sure that the color does not show through to the outside.

2. Place tracing paper between both wrong sides of the garment pieces with the colored sides facing the wrong sides of the fabric.

3. Run the tracing wheel exactly on the lines to be marked. Use a ruler for making straight lines.

4. Remove the pins in one section of the pattern at a time. Trace it. Replace the pins and go to the next section.

5. Mark the three legs of a dart and a short line across the tip to tell you where to stop stitching when you begin to sew. If it is a long fitting dart with two pointed ends, mark it as you would two small darts.

6. Dots are marked with an X.

7. Check to make sure the markings come through on both layers of fabric, but only on the wrong sides.

Complete the following sentences.

4.6 Use _____ tacks and _____ chalk to mark fabric when a tracing wheel cannot be used.

4.7 _____ can be used for marking the placement of trims, hems and alterations.

4.8 The colored sides of the tracing paper should only touch the _____ sides of the fabric.

4.9 Dressmaker's tracing paper is not appropriate for _____ or _____ fabrics.

Complete the following activity.

4.10 Using dressmaker's tracing paper and wheel, practice transferring pattern markings from a pattern to a remnant.

Adult Check _____
Initial   Date

PRESSING

Pressing is flattening a seam or area in order to make it smooth. **Ironing** is to smooth or press clothes with an iron. Pressing and ironing are done in the direction of the grain in order to prevent the fabric from stretching.

Press fabrics before cutting out the pattern if the creases or wrinkles will affect the accuracy of cutting. Test the iron on an inconspicuous part of the garment or fabric sample. Use a light touch and never press over pins.

Plain seams are usually pressed open. Armhole and **design seams** (those seams used for decorative or design purposes) are usually pressed closed. Follow the guide-sheet directions.

Vertical darts are pressed toward center back or center front. Horizontal darts are pressed down toward the hem. On heavy fabric, darts are usually cut on the fold to within one-half inch of each end and pressed open.

Pressing the construction details (seams, darts, etc.) as you finish them helps to give your garment a professional look. Sewing seams is much easier if seams and darts are pressed prior to another seam being stitched over them; for example, pressing the bustline dart before sewing the side seam. If you wait until the garment is entirely finished to do all the inside pressing, the garment will not look as professional as it could. However, leaving the iron on for pressing after completing each step is a tremendous waste of energy. A better procedure would be to sew as much as you can (all darts, seam finishes and no-attaching seams) before heating the iron. Press all of your completed sewing at one time.

 Complete the following activity.

4.11   Lucy is making a simple skirt with side seams and waistline darts.

    a.   How will she press the side seam? _____

    b.   In what direction will she press the darts? _____

    c.   When she is finished, Lucy will press the skirt in the direction of the grain.

       Why? _____

Review the material in this section in preparation for the Self Test. This Self Test will check your mastery of this particular section as well as your knowledge of all previous sections.

SELF TEST 4

Match these fabric terms to the correct section of the diagram (each answer, 4 points).

4.01 _____ bias

4.02 _____ crosswise grain

4.03 _____ raw edges

4.04 _____ lengthwise grain

4.05 _____ selvage

Answer *true* **or** *false* (each answer, 4 points).

4.06 _____ The raw edge of the fabric is called the selvage.

4.07 _____ Extra fabric is needed for plaids, stripes and one-way designs.

4.08 _____ Garments cut off grain will not drape properly on the body.

4.09 _____ The selvage runs parallel to the crosswise threads.

4.010 _____ Keep the fabric flat while you cut.

Complete the following lists (each answer, 4 points).

4.011 Which construction symbols should be transferred from the pattern to the fabric?

a. _____ b. _____

c. _____ d. _____

4.012 What three characteristics does grain perfect fabric have?

a. _____

b. _____

c. _____

4.013 What do you need to know to identify your pattern layout on the guide sheet?

a. _____ b. _____

c. _____

Define the following terms (each answer, 5 points).

4.014 pressing _____

4.015 interfacing _____

4.016 design seam _____

Answer this question (answer, 5 points).

4.017 When should you preshrink your fabric? _____

<table>
<tr><td>80</td></tr>
<tr><td>100</td></tr>
</table>

Score _____

Adult Check _____

Initial   Date

54

V. SEWING PROJECT

SECTION OBJECTIVE

Review this objective. When you have completed this section, you should be able to:

11. Complete a sewing project which demonstrates the knowledge and skills learned.

Pattern. Be careful. Do not select a pattern whose difficulty will discourage you. Finding a pattern with fewer pieces may be helpful, perhaps one labeled "easy to sew" or "jiffy." Be sure the pattern is a style you like, one that looks good on you and is your size. Be sure the pattern reflects the construction methods you've learned.

Fabric. Choose an easily workable fabric such as broadcloth, gingham, or polyester/knit blend. Keep this in mind when selecting a pattern, checking the recommended fabrics on the back of the envelope. Be careful of one-way designs, plaids, and stripes, for they are more challenging to work with. Select a solid fabric or a one that will not have to be matched. Cross reference the view, size, and width of the fabric to determine the amount of fabric which is needed.

Notions. Every pattern will require different notions, but all require matching colored thread. The notions necessary for your pattern are listed on the back of the envelope. Check if your chosen view has additional or different notions. Purchase interfacing if your pattern needs it.

Complete the following activities.

5.1   Choose your pattern. List the following.

    a. company   _____

    b. number   _____

    c. view   _____

    d. size   _____

    e. cost   _____

5.2   Choose your fabric. List the following.

    a. name of fabric   _____

    b. fiber content   _____

    c. shrinkage   _____

    d. care instructions   _____

    e. width   _____

    f. amount   _____

    g. cost   _____

5.3   Choose your notions. List the necessary information.

    a. thread   cost _____

    b. zipper

        size _____   cost _____

    c. elastic

        amount _____

        width _____   cost _____

    d. buttons

        amount _____

        size _____   cost _____

    e. interfacing

        amount _____   cost _____

    f. trim

        amount _____   cost _____

    g. other

        _____   cost _____

        _____   cost _____

    h. total cost of garment
        (add figures in activities
        5.1–5.3)   total cost _____

Adult Check _____

                                                  Initial   **Date**

CONSTRUCTION CHECKLIST

5.4   Follow this checklist in completing your garment. Check each step as you complete it.

_____ Take body measurements in reference to the charts in Section III, page 35 or 36.

_____ Purchase pattern, fabric and notions.

_____ Prepare fabric.

_____ Measure and alter pattern pieces.

    a. Measure the flattened pattern from seam to seam, not including the seam allowance. Remember, the pattern allows a few inches of "ease" (pattern ease) for comfortable fitting.

    b. Since the pattern represents *one-half* of a garment, the measurements (and fabric needed) must be doubled. For example, if a skirt back measures nine inches at the hip and the front measures eight inches, double nine (18) and eight (16). Add the back and front together (18 + 16 = 34) to get the width of the entire skirt.

    c. To lengthen pattern piece, cut the piece in two at alteration line, and then separate it evenly onto tissue paper.

    d. To shorten pattern piece, make an even fold in pattern at alteration line.

    e. To adjust dart location, move its point to the proper location and adjust its legs accordingly.

_____ Lay out and pin pattern.

    a. Circle your layout picture on the guide sheet.

    b. Fold your fabric according to the layout picture.

    c. Place all pattern pieces on the fabric according to the layout picture. Put two pins in each piece—one at each end of the grain-line or the fold-line arrow. Adjust the grain-line arrow so it is parallel to the lengthwise grain. Have an adult check your layout.

    d. Finish pinning your pattern pieces.

    e. Check your work. Compare to your layout diagram.

        1. Do you have all of the necessary pattern pieces? _____

        2. Are the grain line arrows parallel to the selvage? _____

        3. Are the pattern pieces to be placed on the fold exactly even with the fold?

        4. Are the pins across the seam line with the points toward the edge of the pattern? _____

        5. Is a pin in each notch? _____

_____ Have an adult check layout again before cutting.

_____ Cut, mark, and clip pattern/fabric. Clip center front if it is on a fold.

    a. Carefully cut your pattern and fabric. Leave the pattern pinned to the fabric after cutting it out. Throw away small scraps. Save large scraps for sewing and marking practice.

    b. Using dressmaker's tracing paper and wheel, transfer the pattern markings from your pattern to your fabric.

_____ Organize your work. Set goals for unit construction and completion.

_____ Begin sewing according to pattern instructions.

    a. Fill the bobbin with the thread you will be using. Follow the directions in your sewing machine instruction booklet.

    b. Thread the sewing machine.

    c. Test the machine's stitches on a scrap of fabric. Check for correct tension setting and stitch length.

    d. Read and study the guide sheet.

    e. Remove the pattern pieces from the fabric as you use them. Fold each piece and return it to the pattern envelope.

    f. **Stay stitch** your garment pieces according to the directions on the guide sheet.

_____ Read your guide sheet. Usually the next sewing step after stay stitching is sewing the darts. If the garment you are making has darts, stitch them.

_____ Sew the seams of your garment as directed in your guide sheet. Select one of the seam finishes and finish the seams of your garment.

_____ Be sure to try on your garment several times during construction to check fit.

_____ If your garment calls for a zipper, insert it now.

_____ With the help of your guide sheet, attach the facings to your garment.

_____ If you are making a garment with a waistband, try it on and check the fit. Use your guide sheet for instructions on how to adjust and make a waistband. Make any adjustment. Stitch the waistband to your garment.

_____ If you are making a garment with a casing, with the help of your guide sheet make your casing.

_____ Read your guide sheet. Make sure that all steps are completed up to the hem. **Press your garment.**

_____ Hem your garment.

    a. Try your garment on and have a partner mark the hem for you.

    b. Follow the steps in this LIFEPAC for pinning your hem.

    c. Try on your garment and check the evenness of the length and hems.

    d. Hand stitch or machine stitch your hem.

_____ Add the finishing touches: buttons, buttonholes, snaps, hooks and eyes, etc.

_____ Final pressing.

_____ Evaluate and submit to an adult for a grade.

SEWING EVALUATION FORM

Name _____ Date _____

Type of garment _____

1 = very well done

2 = satisfactory

3 = needs improvement

To be filled out by both the student and the teacher.

	Student	Teacher
General Appearance		
Pattern suits the student		
Fabric suits the pattern		
Fabric suits the student		
Choice of thread		
Choice of trim		
Neatness		
Fit on student		
Sewing Preparation		
Fabric grain line perfect		
Pattern pieces cut on grain		
Notches cut away from seam allowance		
Pattern symbols transferred to fabric correctly		
Garment Construction		
Stay stitching		
Darts		
a. Ends in a fine point		
b. Bust darts point to the fullest part of the bust (ladies only)		
c. Darts opposite each other are equal in length and width		
d. Pressed in correct direction		

Tucks, pleats, gathers

    a. Tucks stitched even and straight; look uniform and neat, pressed correctly

    b. Pleats accurately aligned and pressed

    c. Gathers are even and fit the adjoining edge

Seams

    a. Stitching straight

    b. Seam allowance even

    c. Pressed correctly

    d. Neatly finished

    e. Top-stitching straight

    f. Top stitching even

Zippers

    a. Stitching straight and parallel to the seam

    b. Zipper does not show when garment is worn

Facings, neck and armhole

    a. Curve clipped, facing lies flat

    b. Seam allowance graded or trimmed, no bulk

    c. Edge stitching or another clean finish

    d. Under-stitching done neatly

    e. Neckline interfaced correctly

    f. Seam even at zipper opening

Waistband

    a. Correctly interfaced

    b. Same width the entire length

    c. Hand stitches do not show on outside

    d. Even seam at waistline

    e. Snug closing

Casing

    a. Folded evenly

    b. Stitching straight

    c. Elastic smooth, not twisted

    d. Gathers distributed evenly

Finishing Touches

Hem

    a. Parallel to the floor

    b. Uniform in width

    c. Edge stitching straight

    d. Seam binding applied neatly

Buttons and button holes

    a. Thread shank, if needed

b. Place correctly		
c. Small, neat stitches		
d. Buttonholes should have two even parallel rows of zigzag stitching with bar tack at ends		
Hooks and eyes		
a. Placed correctly		
b. Small, neat stitches		
c. No stitches show on outside		
Snaps		
a. Placed correctly		
b. Small neat stitches		
c. No stitches show on outside		
General		
a. Unneeded visible threads removed		
b. Well pressed, but not over-pressed		
c. Clean and ready to wear		

General Comments

Work habits		
Project turned in on time		
Effort		
Gets along with others		

Student's comments _____

_____

_____

_____

Teacher's comments _____

_____

_____

_____

Score _____

Adult Check _____
Initial   Date

GLOSSARY

allowance. Distance between the cutting line and seam line.

bias. Diagonal grain line formed when the lengthwise thread is folded parallel to the crosswise thread; has stretch.

bobbin. Spool-like thread holder that supplies bottom thread for sewing machines.

burr. A rough edge left on a needle through prolonged use.

bonded fabric. Fabric that has a lining-like fabric attached to the wrong side.

clip. To trim by cutting. To cut or cut off or out, as with shears.

dart. A short, tapered, stitched area that enables the garment to fit the figure.

design seam. An extra seam added to give a detail or design a look to the garment. ex: a yoke seam.

facing. Fabric used to finish raw edges at garment openings, such as neck or armholes.

filling grains. The crosswise grain going from selvage to selvage across the fabric.

gathering. Pulling an amount of fabric into a smaller area along a stitch to create soft, even folds.

grade. Trimming all of a seam's allowances to different widths in order to eliminate bulk. The interfacing allowance is always trimmed close to the seam.

grain. The direction of the lengthwise and crosswise threads in fabric. Threads should be perpendicular to each other.

grain perfect. When the crosswise threads are at a ninety degree angle to the lengthwise threads.

interfacing. A third layer of fabric used for shaping the garment.

ironing. The smoothing or pressing of clothes with an iron.

marking. Transferring construction symbols from the pattern to the material.

napped fabric. Fabric with a raised surface such as corduroy and velvet; when used, all pattern pieces must be laid in the same direction. Often, more fabric is needed than the pattern actually calls for. (also referred to as "with nap")

notions. The extra sewing supplies, other than the fabric, needed to complete the garment: zipper, buttons, thread, etc.

one-way design. A print pattern that noticeably goes in only one direction. More fabric is required to place all the pattern pieces in the same direction.

pivot. With the presser foot lifted and the needle still in the fabric, turning the fabric to a desired angle.

placket. The opening or slit at the top of a garment that facilitates putting it on and taking it off.

pleats. Folds in fabric which provide a controlled fullness.

preshrink. Shrinking the material before it is used to make a garment.

pressing. The flattening of a seam in order to make it smooth.

raw edge. Where the fabric has been cut; woven material unravels at the raw edge.

right. The side of the fabric that is meant to be seen.

seam. Where two pieces of fabric are sewn together.

selvage. The woven edge of the fabric, parallel to the lengthwise grain.

shuttle. The sliding bobbin container in a sewing machine.

stay stitching. A line of machine stitches shown on first part of a pattern instructions, generally for beginning stages of garment only. Stay stitching is done in the direction of the grain of fabric and $1/8''$ away from seam line.

tracing paper and **tracing wheel.** A method of marking fabric by using a type of carbon paper and a sharpened wheel to transfer pattern directions.

trim. To cut away excess fabric from an allowance after the seam has been stitched.

tuck. A stitched fold of fabric for decorative or shaping purposes.

warp. Lengthwise threads of woven fabrics.

woof. Crosswise threads of woven fabrics.

wrong. The side of the fabric that is not meant to be seen.

BIBLIOGRAPHY

Reader's Digest *Complete Guide to Sewing,* 11th printing, The Reader's Digest Association, Inc., New York, 1985.

Saunders, Jan, *Sewing for Dummies*, IDG Books Worldwide, Inc., Foster City, CA, 1999.

Singer Sewing Reference Library, *Clothing Care and Repair*, Cy DeCrosse Incorporated, Minnesota, 1985.

The Vogue Sewing Book, Butterick Publishing, New York, 1980.

Wagenvoord, James, Personal Style, *The Man's Guide to Fashion, Fitness, Travel and Entertaining,* Holt, Rinehart and Winston, New York, 1985.

NOTES